THE ART
AND SCIENCE OF
CLICKER TRAINING
FOR HORSES

THE ART
AND SCIENCE OF
CLICKER TRAINING
FOR HORSES

*A Positive Approach to training equines
and understanding them*

BEN HART

SOUVENIR PRESS

CONTENTS

LIST OF ILLUSTRATIONS

ACKNOWLEDGEMENTS

This book is the result of ten years of clicker training, therefore, a huge thank you must go to the horses, donkeys and mules I have worked with in this time. Their owners concerns and questions have inspired this book and are the basis for the way in which it is written. Thank you to The Donkey Sanctuary, for their kind permission to reproduce the photos of Cocoa H, Mrs Knox and Jack M. I am very grateful to Nic Barker and Andy Willis for allowing Bailey and Charlie to be used as such willing photographic models. I greatly appreciate the help, support and patience of everyone at Souvenir Press and to Colin Murry for his patience with editing the manuscript twice. I truly value the encouragement I have received, from clients, family and friends, Thank you all.

Finally, to my partner Canny, whose impeccable timing and observational skills as a trainer, have taken clicker training to a new level. I cannot thank her enough for her belief in my writing and training skills, her editorial support and her patience throughout this whole process.

ACKNOWLEDGMENTS

*This book is dedicated in memory of my father,
a man who was ahead of his time.*

INTRODUCTION

My character is such that when I stumbled across Karen Pryor's book *Don't Shoot the Dog*, in 1998, I spent several months researching, questioning and testing the possibilities and potential for using this method of training with horses. I wanted to be sure it could be safely used with equines. From there, I was, I believe, the first trainer in the UK to include clicker training in the syllabus of workshops and clinics. Then there have been years of teaching and using clicker training with equines but, despite requests for written information and books, I have waited to write this book about clicker training because it has taken until now to perfect the art and science of clicker training equines.

I have always felt that clicker training has been taken too lightly by enthusiast and sceptic alike. I have never believed that just clicking and rewarding is all there is to clicker training. I have felt that there has been something more to learn before I could give the complete picture of clicker training. Now I feel I have learnt what I believe to be the missing pieces of the jigsaw and I want to share my knowledge for the benefit of current clicker trainers, potential clicker trainers and the animals themselves. However, I also want the method of clicker training itself to be understood and used well, so that it can benefit many horses, donkeys and mules for as long as possible. This book is the truth about clicker training horses, donkeys and mules

The book is based around the most common questions I am asked about clicker training and the most common problems I see trainers experience. I have included sections on how I start to use clicker training, how I remove the clicker as a guide and how I apply the principles of behaviour to practical horsemanship. Clicker training is based on the science of learning and if we understand that science we can understand the importance and potential of clicker training. Instead of the labels of magical and miracle, the truth is found in the science of learning and its careful application.

Most importantly for me, I have placed the clicker in the context of the science of behaviour and horsemanship by not continuing the magical clicker myth or subscribing to the realms of one size fits all solutions. Clicker training has become decoupled from horsemanship and I do not think that should be the case, so I have taken the science of behaviour and the art of horsemanship and put clicker training in the context of our communication with our animals.

This book is written for trainers of horses, donkeys and mules because, using the science of behaviour, it is possible to train them all using clicker training. This is not normally the case for an equine training method. Throughout the book I use the term animal, rather than horse so as not to differentiate between horses, donkeys and mules. By using the term animal, I hope that readers will recognise that I am trying to show that the correct use of clicker training can benefit horses, donkey and mules.

It is my belief that whenever anyone interacts with an equine in any way, they teach it something. For this reason I use the term trainer to describe anyone who is interacting with the animal. Often the word trainer is reserved for those people who make their living from professionally training equines. Owners, riders, grooms or helpers often do not realise they too are trainers. Throughout this book I have used the word trainer in this way rather than make any distinction between different labels people give themselves for their roles in their equine relationships.

Whether you are an existing clicker trainer or just starting out with clicker training, this book clarifies the grey areas and shows how the application of the science of behaviour can create effective, safe clicker training for horses, donkeys and mules.

CHAPTER 1

What's the fuss about?

The clicker has been portrayed by some horse trainers as a magic solution to every imaginable horse problem and, excitingly, the method has that potential. However, this claim of infallibility is the biggest danger to the success of clicker training as an equine training method. Clicker training is often sold as an easy, quick fix and a positive method through which anyone and every equine can succeed. If it were that simple, horses all over the world would have their lives transformed and many behaviourists would happily be out of business because there would be the wonderful situation of no more problem horses to "fix".

I believe that clicker training does have fantastic potential to transform equine training, but only if people see that it works. If its use is oversimplified and incorrect training causes it to be ineffective, the horse world will throw the clicker in the back of the tack box along with all the other gadgets and equipment that have failed the horse enthusiast in the last twenty years.

Clicker training has been marketed as the only 100 per cent positive training method for equines, and it has been labelled as the magic modern way to train any animal to do anything. But are these claims true? Is clicker training magic or is it just another method of training that some smart horse trainer or scientist came up with in order to make money? To understand whether all of the claims about clicker training are realistic, we need to ask a few questions.

The first question we can ask to gain an insight into the true potential of the clicker is, "can clicker training stop a bolting horse?' The answer is, "Not while they are bolting!" Given that bolting is most often caused by fear and that the animal is running in flat out panic, it would be extremely unlikely that a bolting horse would come gently to a stop on the chance they may receive a small piece of carrot as a reward for stopping. If, however, we ask if we can we use clicker training to retrain a horse that bolts, the answer is that we can.

Can we really stop a horse from biting just by clicking and giving them some food? Well, the answer is yes we can, but, and it is a very big but, it is not as simple as it sounds. The cause of the biting must first be established, the trainer must understand how behaviours are created and changed and the trainer's timing needs to be impeccable if clicker training is to be successful each and every time it is used.

As with all methods of training the clicker is a training aid and it is only as good as the hands that operate it. A clicker does not teach a horse anything. The operator of the clicker teaches and the clicker simply aids the skill of the operator in conveying the message accurately to the animal. So, unfortunately, a poor trainer will still only have limited success with the clicker, while a talented one will make it seem like the magic pill of training equines.

The truth is that no part of horsemanship can be considered in isolation and clicker training is still subject to the science and laws of learning and behaviour. Just because a trainer uses a clicker, the other rules and laws of behaviour and training are not abandoned. How the horse learns and behaves still has to be thoroughly understood before repeated successes with a variety of equines can be expected.

Not only does clicker training have the potential to train equines in a positive and ethical way, it also has the potential to make the equine world look at its other accepted methods of training and to cause individual trainers to look at their own beliefs about how equines should be treated. Clicker training could also transform how we think about the learning abilities and the intelligence of our equines. A tiny plastic and metal box that makes a clicking noise holds huge potential for increasing our knowledge of how equines learn. What a great shame if this opportunity to enter a new world of equine understanding was lost for the sake of honesty about the limitations of clicker training and the truth about what it really takes to make the clicker work to its full potential.

The impressive "miracles" of animal training that have been attributed to clicker training are an extremely compelling argument for the cure all, magical attributes that are often attached to the clicker.

One of the most public and well known areas of clicker success has been in marine animal shows, where the tremendous feats of dolphins and killer whales have amazed and thrilled audiences around the world. The marine animal training world has been using the science of clicker training, albeit with a whistle not a clicker, for about forty years. Perhaps this simple substitution of tools gives us the first real evidence that clickers are not magic – well not unless whistles are too, and as yet I have not heard of magic whistle training. Nevertheless, the training of dolphins, whales, sea lions and seals through operant conditioning has demonstrated the potential of using clicker training to train large and potentially dangerous mammals.

The canine world has benefited from a touch of "clicker magic", with thousands of trainers converting to the use of positive reinforcement and clicker training. As a result, dogs have been shown to learn faster and more enthusiastically than ever seen before.

Zoo animals around the world have also reaped the rewards of the clicker. Keepers have used the science of clicker training to put on shows and train the behaviour of their animals to aid welfare and husbandry practices.

One of the clearest examples of the effectiveness of clicker training comes from San Diego Zoo. The zoo's aggressive bull elephant was shaped, using clicker training, to place his feet through a hole in a metal gate so they could be trimmed for the first time in ten years. Following that, he was trained to place an ear through the hole so that the keepers could take blood samples safely, thus allowing them to check on the health of his internal organs. What is even more amazing is that, as his training progressed, this elephant became less aggressive and safer to be around. This was all achieved with just carrots, a clicker and the skill and ability of the trainers.

Around the world, zoos and wildlife parks have trained all manner of birds to create informative and entertaining shows. Parrots that cycle, roller skate, and recycle rubbish into bins are motivated to work with food, and the message of successful behaviour is conveyed to the bird using the sound of the clicker.

Film makers have not been slow to capitalise on the capacity of clicker training to train a wide range of animals and birds for the movie sets and television studios of the world. The pigs from the film *Babe*, the zebra used in the film *Racing Stripes* , sheep, geese, dogs, cats and the owl in the Harry Potter films, to name just a few, have all demonstrated the success of clicker training.

Other animals that have been clicker trained include rabbits, cats, llamas and even exotic species such as iguanas. I have even seen a wild robin turn circles on the edge of a bucket for a click and reward of meal worms.

So, given this incredible record of success, it is only natural that enthusiastic trainers will make incredible claims for the unlimited possibilities of clicker training with equines. The possibility of positive reinforcement as an equine training method was first brought to the forefront by natural horse trainers and, stimulated by this evolution in horsemanship, owners have begun to look for kinder, more empathetic ways to train horses. Clicker training and its dangling carrot of 100 per cent positive training has been an irresistible draw.

Among some of its advocates, the magical clicker has

been promoted to almost iconic status. This enthusiasm is in part because so many equine owners are keen to be loved by their horses. Any method of training that is likely to increase the horse's "affection" towards their human is bound to be popular.

On the positive side, clicker training has created a new imagination for the potential of equine intelligence. The tricks and behaviours that were seldom dreamt of, except on film sets, have suddenly become accessible to the ordinary horse owner. Horses playing football, retrieving objects, bowing and interacting with owners have given the horse owner somewhere else to go with the horse/human relationship.

Despite the excitement of those who believe clicker training equines is the only way to train horses, donkeys and mules, its advance into the equine world has been somewhat slower than in the dog world. Although advocates of the method have demonstrated its effectiveness by showing horses doing all sorts of tricks that before clicker training would not have been considered possible, let alone ethical, the method has not been taken to the core of the training beliefs as it has been in other species.

The advocates of clicker training tell of the amazing behaviours that can be taught with clicker training. In fact, everything from a goldfish swimming through hoops, and horses trained to act as guide dogs have been clicker trained. These achievements are very impressive, but we still have to consider whether it is the clicker that trains the animal or whether it is the way the trainer uses it that creates the learning. If you place a clicker on the stable wall or in the cage it will not train the animal to do anything. Only when the trainer picks up the clicker with their hands and use their brains do the amazing feats of learning happen.

At first glance it may appear, to the clicker sceptic, that clicker training is only good for tricks, or perhaps best for species that are easily motivated by food. It is still widely held that equines won't work for food rewards because they are prey animals not predators, or that food rewards will just teach equines to bite. Neither of these myths is true.

There can be no doubt that positive reinforcement in the form of clicker training has been a success with many equines. I personally have used it with aggressive horses, kicking donkeys and nervous mules. On the World Wide Web there are thousands of pictures of horses standing on boxes, walking over obstacles, putting balls in baskets and bowing, all trained with a clicker.

I was grateful for the potential of the clicker when I found myself on a flooded island with a donkey called Swifty. Swifty was in his early twenties and had spent all but the first six months of his life on a small island, in a lake complex just outside London. During a very wet autumn the water levels began to rise and eventually began to flood the island. Despite attempts by rescue organisations and six firemen pulling on a lead rope, Swifty was determined to remain in his home.

As a last resort, I had been asked to try to handle this supposedly difficult donkey and get him off the island before the flood water covered it completely. I set to work using an empty drink bottle as an improvised target, my clicker and the donkey's favourite reward, ginger biscuits. I had to train the donkey to lead, overcome his fear of water and follow me through a narrow gap in a fence to high ground. It did take several hours to complete the rescue, but after twenty years with no training or handling and after the failure of pure strength to overpower Swifty, clicker training proved its worth.

What was more amazing was that once on dry land I had to load Swifty into a trailer for the final leg of the journey to safety. Despite his ordeal, a film crew, twenty bystanders and only ever having been on a trailer once, Swifty's courage and clicker training meant he followed me on to the trailer in just a couple of minutes and all with a minimum of stress.

I have even used clicker training in emergency situations. During a visit to a farm, I arrived to discover a distraught horse owner with a beautiful chestnut mare whose leg was badly cut. The owner had called the vet but was now starting to worry as the mare did not have a good reputation with vets and veterinary procedures. When asked to assist I offered to try and use clicker training to help the mare deal with the situation. I spent twenty minutes before the vet's arrival working with the mare and, despite the discomfort, she learnt to stand still and allowed me to examine the leg and pretend to give her a sedative injection. Despite breaking my own rules on the use of clicker training with pain and in non clicker trained animals she still learnt to stand and relax. The mare accepted the vet and was willing to stand to have the sedation injection which, prior to the clicker training, would have been a dangerous and stressful procedure.

So clicker training does work with equines, but is all the hype and promise of a magic pill for all equine problems really justifiable? Clicker training seems to be advocated in all situations, with any ability of trainer, for all difficulties. Unfortunately, there is a growing number of stories of horses becoming over-excited and frustrated during the clicker training process. Certain trainers have reported horses becoming more food possessive, developing mugging behaviour and becoming sexually excited during the training sessions.

It would seem to me that clicker training has incredible potential and it does work really well. However, it is far from magic. Successful clicker training requires practical skill on the part of the trainer and understanding of the science of behaviour. Perhaps the biggest threat to the longevity of clicker training is the over simplification of its principles. Making clicker training more appealing by simplifying the process allows well meaning people to show the potential of the clicker and advocate its use with all equines all of the time and by anyone. This almost evangelical approach is clearly dangerous.

Throughout the chapters of this book I want to look at the truth about the practical application of clicker training. Using the science of clicker training identically between different species without making some fundamental changes in the approaches to compensate for species specific behaviour and motivational differences could be the downfall of a great equine training tool. Clicker training is really quite simple, but only if the trainers know what they are doing, and have the skills and knowledge to use the clicker correctly.

Many descriptions of how to get started with clicker training and how to train using it are a couple of pages long. Unfortunately, it is not that simple. Clicker training cannot make up for a lack of equine training skills or a personal deficit of knowledge on equine behaviour. However, when clicker training is used correctly and with understanding, it can open up a channel of communication that has never previously existed between equines and humans, and that truly is its greatest gift.

CHAPTER 2

What exactly is clicker training?

In the most simplistic terms, clicker training is a way of rewarding good behaviour very accurately. Once established, the process is very simple; press the clicker at the appropriate moment and then offer a reward and the animal understands which behaviour is being reinforced. Unfortunately, the scientific process that establishes the link between noise, reward and behaviour is more complicated.

Trying to define what clicker training actually is provides us with a challenge between the complex scientific terminology and a more simplified but less descriptive explanation. Clicker training could be described as a method of animal training that uses a small plastic box containing a metal strip, the clicker, to influence the behaviour of the animal being trained. To put it a slightly more descriptive way, clicker training is a method of training using positive reinforcement to encourage desired behaviour in the trainee. If we try to provide a scientific explanation we get something like this: clicker training is a method of increasing the desired behaviour of the trainee by the use of positive reinforcement through operant conditioning and using a conditioned reinforcer as a bridging stimulus to improve the timing between a behaviour and the delivery of a primary reinforcer.

I believe that it is extremely helpful to the trainer to understand the processes of learning that are involved in the science of clicker training because this understanding underpins the process of teaching clicker training to any animal. Understanding the science helps to prevent many of the pitfalls of clicker training, and therefore speeds up the process of learning in the equine and the trainer.

There are various scientific elements that we must look at to get the full picture of what is happening when we use clicker training. These areas include classical conditioning, operant conditioning, positive reinforcement, primary and secondary reinforcers. It must be noted that scientists studying the science of behaviour are still learning about the connection between the different aspects of classical and operant conditioning and the subject is enormous and the terminology quite complicated. Entire books have been written on each element, which is why clicker training is often over-simplified. Any attempt to define the science of the processes involved is difficult. However, accurate simplification can really help the clicker trainer to improve their understanding of the process.

Classical conditioning

The process of classical conditioning is also known as Pavlovian conditioning after the Russian scientist who discovered it. The term "conditioning" or "conditioned" in this scientific sense simply means learning or learnt.

Ivan Pavlov (1849-1936) founded the Institute of Experimental Medicine in 1890 and he studied digestion. In 1901, in the now famous experiments, Pavlov noted that while testing dogs for saliva production, the dogs began to produce saliva at the sight of the lab technicians who were about to feed them.

In Pavlov's experiments, dogs were harnessed in a sound and smell-proof cubical so they could not hear, see or smell the technicians. A sound was made when meat powder was fed to the dogs and their salivation measured. After several pairings or trials, the sound without the food was given, but the dogs still salivated. The dogs had been conditioned to associate the sound with the presentation of the food. As far as their immediate physiological responses were concerned, the sound became equivalent to the presentation of the food. Classical conditioning explains most learning that involves reflexes such as heart rate, salivation, perspiration, emotional responses, muscle tension or eye blinks etc.

Before commencing clicker training, the click means nothing to the animal. It is a neutral stimulus, unless of course the animal is afraid of the noise, in which case it is a negative stimulus, the effects of which must be overcome to continue training. The click represents the sound in Pavlov's experiment. Only by repeated pairing with a primary reinforcer does the click begin to have any meaning to the animal. I start the animal with simple behaviours such as targeting or standing still to meet the need for this conditioning between the click and the reinforcer, which is essential for clicker training to be effective. Often trainers talk about charging the clicker. Usually this is achieved by random clicking and offering of rewards, in order to pair the noise and the food together. I personally find that while this method can work, it is not as effective at teaching the animal the "rules" of clicker training as teaching a very simple task to make the association. Whatever way is chosen, it is a mistake to purchase a clicker and immediately start clicker training the horse to perform a difficult behaviour or overcome a behavioural problem.

Classical conditioning can occur in many circumstances, whether intended by the trainer or not. If during initial exposure to a novel object when out hacking, the horse is smacked with a whip or kicked in the ribs repeatedly to make them go past the object, the object can become associated to the pain of smacks or kicks. This association will mean that future exposure to the object will elicit the fear/pain response without the horse being smacked. Breeding stallions can become conditioned to their breeding bridles. If the same bridle is used each time the animal is taken to cover a mare, the sight of the bridle will soon produce a sexual response in the stallion. Horses that wear ill fitting tack which causes pain will soon associate that tack with pain and the sight of the tack will produce muscle tension. This is then considered a conditioned emotional response.

An unconditioned stimulus is essentially anything that the animal does not have to learn how to respond to, such as a loud noise, pain, bright light, food, sex etc. The unconditioned stimulus will reliably produce a response without the need for any conditioning. A conditioned stimulus on the other hand is anything which produces a response as a result of conditioning. Prior to conditioning the stimulus did not produce the new response, although it might have produced other responses. These are events that start off with no meaning or different meanings and, as a result of pairing with an unconditioned stimulus, take on a new meaning to the animal. So, in our examples, the pain inflicted is an unconditioned stimulus and the object encountered while riding becomes a conditioned stimulus so that in future the object will produce the fear response. The smell or sight of a mare in season is an unconditioned stimulus and the breeding bridle becomes a conditioned stimulus when used for mating only. The food used in clicker training is an unconditioned stimulus, and the click becomes a conditioned stimulus when repeatedly paired with the food.

The key to classical conditioning is simply the pairing of two events, typically one after the other. One event must be an unconditioned stimulus for the other event to become a conditioned stimulus. The new conditioned stimulus precedes the unconditioned stimulus.

Interestingly, scratches and human touch are an unconditioned stimulus. Naturally, the touch of a human produces a fear response in a foal or unhandled equine, and this fear is unconditioned. Only after repeated use and eventual pairing with relaxation can a stroke or a scratch produce a calming effect, and then the human touch becomes a conditioned stimulus. Equines that have not had exposure to this form of classical conditioning will not find the human touch calming or reinforcing.

Once classical conditioning has taken place, the conditioned stimulus produces a predictable response that it did not previously produce. This new response is called a conditioned response. The animal has to learn what the click means. So the click, through repeated pairing with food, begins to produce the same reflex action as the sight of food. In the case of clicker training, it becomes a reliable predictor that food is coming. In fact, in experiments the conditioned stimulus takes on the reinforcing properties of the unconditioned stimulus. In this case, the click could take on the reinforcing properties of the food. However, if a conditioned stimulus is consistently presented without the unconditioned stimulus, reduction of the conditioned response will occur. Simply put, if you keep repeatedly clicking and stop giving any food, the click will stop producing the same response as food, and the click will lose its value.

The conditioned response does not start out strong or happen instantly. It is a process of learning and the best way to begin this process will be the subject of the chapter "How do I get started?"

Reinforcement

We are beginning to see that the equine must learn about the meaning of the click before clicker training can start in earnest. But how do we turn this conditioned stimulus into a useful training tool? To do this we need to understand how the clicker, once conditioned, can be used to increase behaviour and to do that we need to understand the process of reinforcement.

A reinforcer is anything that will increase the likelihood of a behaviour recurring when it is produced, removed or cancelled following that behaviour. The procedure of reinforcement is the arranging of the relationship between a behaviour and a reinforcer. Reinforcement can be either positive, through the addition of something the animal considers positive, such as food, or negative, through the removal of something the animal considers negative, such as pressure.

Food is considered a primary reinforcer because equines do not have to learn that food is valuable and it can function as a reinforcer with little previous experience. One of the early oppositions to the use of clicker training with equines was that they were not motivated by food because food was constantly available to them in the wild, and that therefore they did not develop the motivation to work for food that predators have. While this argument may have some sound reasoning, one only has to look at the competition between horses for food when it is scarce to know that they will work for food when it is in short supply. The reason that food works as a reinforcer in domesticated equines is because we constantly restrict the type and variety of their diet. This restriction in volume and variety means that our domestic equines can be motivated by novel foods. Obviously, using handfuls of grass to clicker train a horse while standing in a field full of the stuff might produce limited results. In contrast, the use of novel and restricted feeds such as vegetables, fruit, purposely designed treats, high-fibre products, even fresh grass if the animal does not have access to grass, can have a very motivating result. However, the deliberate restriction of the horse's food ration in an attempt to increase the animal's motivation is not necessary and may even be considered unethical.

The difficulty of using food as a reinforcer is delivering the food with the correct timing so that the animal understands which particular behaviour is the one which receives rewards. For example, if we are using food rewards to teach a donkey to pick up a foot, once the foot has been lifted we generally have to put it down and return to the head of the animal in order to administer the food. This delay in the arrival of the food can cause confusion as to which behaviour is being reinforced.

The ability to accurately mark one element of a desired behaviour is particularly difficult to do using just food due to the poor timing of the delivery of the reward.

To cancel out the effect of poor timing of the food reward, the trainer can use a conditioned reinforcer, also known as a secondary reinforcer. A secondary reinforcer is something that gains its ability to act as a reinforcer through experience, especially as a result of classical conditioning. Events become secondary reinforcers when they predict the occurrence of primary reinforcers. Hence our click is paired with food and, through experience, the equine learns that a click means food is coming. This ability of the click to predict the delivery of food causes the click to become a secondary reinforcer.

The easiest way to understand a secondary reinforcer is to think of money. Money is not something that human beings are born understanding or having a desire for. Money has value because of the things for which it can be exchanged, such as food, shelter, entertainment, water etc. School or university grades are another example of secondary reinforcers. Grades only have value because of what they can bring and we learn through experience that grade A can bring praise from teachers and parents, career opportunities, university places and good jobs while grade E brings detention, punishment, poor prospects and criticism.

Secondary reinforcers have some important attributes, such as their exchange rate. Money is valued by what you can exchange it for. In clicker training the value of the click relates to the value the animal places on the food reward or scratch. Secondly, and very importantly, a secondary reinforcer can be given immediately but not exchanged for something until later. In clicker training, the click is given but the reward may not arrive until several seconds later, but the click retains its status as a reinforcer despite the delay. In this way, secondary reinforcers can bridge the time between the occurrence of a behaviour and the delivery of the primary reinforcer. This single fact is the reason why clicker training has so much potential to aid the communication between human and equine during training.

One would think that producing the food and the click together would be the best way to pair the two, but this is not necessarily the case. If two stimuli are presented together, one may overshadow the other. The stronger one, in this case the food, may dominate or overshadow the click, so that the click is hardly perceived. Therefore, we condition the click by clicking first and then producing the food reward. Many first time clicker trainers get the reward out of the bum bag and have it in their hand ready to give to the animal because they think it should be given immediately after the click. The obvious sight and smell of food rewards may overshadow the click, thereby slowing the learning process. When we start pairing food and click, we leave the reward in the bum bag until after the click has been given to avoid overshadowing.

The strength of a secondary reinforcer is measured by how well it can increase the probability of a behaviour recurring. The strength of the secondary reinforcer is determined by the number of times it is paired with the primary reinforcer, the quantity and value of the primary reinforcer as well as the length of delay between the secondary reinforcer and the primary reinforcer. So we can see clicker training involves the establishment of a link between primary and secondary reinforcers to help bridge the gap between behaviour and reward But what is a reward and what effects does it have on learning?

Operant conditioning

This type of learning was established and researched by B. F. Skinner and differs from classical conditioning in that it works on non-reflexive or voluntary behaviour. The term operant is used because the animal is considered to operate on its environment. Operant conditioning is sometimes also called instrumental learning because the animal's behaviour is considered instrumental in their own learning how to obtain reinforcement.

There are several elements of operant conditioning, the most familiar are punishment, negative reinforcement and positive reinforcement. Each of these operant responses can only be understood by understanding the consequences they produce. If, for example, one horse approaches too close behind another and is kicked, the pain of the kick should decrease the likelihood of the horse approaching too closely again. This relationship between behaviour and future decreasing of the behaviour is known as punishment. A punisher is anything that is likely to reduce or diminish the chances of a particular behaviour happening again in the future.

If the consequences of a behaviour are the removal or cessation of an existing negative or unpleasant stimulus, such as the removal of the pressure from the rider's spurs as the horse speeds up, then the relationship between behaviour and consequence is know as negative reinforcement. Negative reinforcement will increase the future likelihood of the behaviour, in this case moving faster, happening again in response to the same stimulus.

Positive reinforcement is a consequence that increases the likelihood of a behaviour recurring, if it is presented during or immediately following the behaviour. A positive reinforcer is something that an individual will seek out and is more commonly known as a reward. So for equines, food, water, mutual grooming, companionship and freedom may all be considered positive reinforcers.

During positive reinforcement a horse is more likely to receive rewards for performing a desired behaviour than if they perform undesired behaviours. If an equine can establish a link between their behaviour and positive consequences for that behaviour they are more likely to repeat the behaviour in the hope of receiving a reward. Simple really. If you like the consequences of what you do, you are more likely to do it again.

If the horse nibbles at the bolt on the field gate and accidentally opens the gate, their nibbling has been rewarded with freedom, provided of course that the horse views freedom from the field as positive. If the horse wants or enjoys their freedom, then the nibbling behaviour is likely to be repeated. If a donkey is kicking the stable door when the owner arrives with carrots, the donkey will learn the accidental association between kicking the door and the reward of carrots, and door kicking will increase. If a mule allows themselves to be caught easily and receives a handful of high fibre nuts once the head collar is on, the likelihood is they will increase the behaviour of approaching the owner and being caught, but only if they like fibre nuts! If a mule is bribed with a handful of high fibre nuts and given a few for just reaching with a long neck from as far away as possible, it will learn to repeat the behaviour of stretching its neck and snatching the reward and running away. Positive reinforcement is the element of operant conditioning that clicker training uses to increase the chances of reinforced behaviours happening again.

It is important to remember that it is the animal's perception of the event, not the trainer's intention, which determines if an event is positive, negative or punishment for the animal. A trainer may intend a scratch on the withers for standing still to be positive, but if the horse is afraid or in pain then scratches are likely to be perceived as punishment for standing still. Carrots are not positive to a donkey if they do not like them, or they have already eaten too many.

The term operant conditioning refers to the fact that the learner changes their environment through their own learning. By offering behaviours, and understanding the consequences of those behaviours, an animal can choose which behaviours they perform to reproduce the consequences they desire. Once an equine has learnt that a click is a good thing because it predicts that food will arrive, they can begin to offer behaviours in the hope of receiving a click and therefore a primary reinforcer.

However, at this point, the individual distinctiveness of the animal determines the rate of learning.

A common mistake with clicker training is to believe that it is a cure all and that all equines will enjoy it and learn quickly. The speed of learning will be in large part down to the nature of the animal. The nervous horse that has previously been punished for mistakes will be more timid and reserved in offering behaviours for fear of the consequences of their behaviour. An individual who is confident, has been encouraged to think and has not been punished for mistakes will be much more likely to offer a wider range of behaviours. The more behaviours the animal offers, the more behaviours a trainer has to select from, thereby increasing the amount of reinforcement the animal receives. This increased reinforcement speeds up the learning process.

Reinforcement can be viewed as providing the animal with information on which behaviours are effective at receiving rewards. The more accurate the information which the equine receives the easier it will be for them to understand and offer the required behaviour. As we will see later, the provision of information can lead to overloading. Clicking for every tiny behaviour that the horse offers will provide very little usable information and, although the animal may enjoy being fed, learning will be slow and frustrating.

Operant conditioning is a very powerful process of equine learning. It occurs with or without the trainer's knowledge. By understanding the science of operant conditioning we are better able to understand elements of clicker training, such as free shaping and the effects of positive reinforcement on learning. In fact, understanding operant conditioning is to understand much of the science of clicker training

As we begin to understand the science behind the process of using secondary reinforcers we can use the information to provide more accurate training and to use clicker training very effectively. For clicker training to work to its full potential we have to accept it is not a tool we can buy from the tack shop in the morning and use it to solve the horse's problems in the afternoon. It takes time to establish the clicker as a secondary reinforcer and for the animal to learn that they are now expected to offer behaviours for which they can gain food. Equines have to learn the rules and etiquette for clicker training safely, just as the trainer has to learn how to operate this new technology and juggle the target, the equine, the clicker and food rewards with only two hands.

Sometimes, because they love the positive nature of clicker training, new converts to clicker training overreach themselves and, in their enthusiasm, begin to train any and every animal they come across. The science of the clicker does not replace the practical horsemanship that is required to safely handle equines. The trainer needs to observe the animal's body language and still be conscious of their own. The trainer has to use successive approximation well, have confidence, trust, and be able to sympathetically handle the animal. My golden rule for trainers is, if they do not have the skills and experience to work safely with a problem equine or a problem behaviour without clicker training, then they should not try and work with the problem using clicker training.

Clicker training requires a mix of classical and operant conditioning to establish a connection between primary and secondary reinforcers which are then used to bridge the gap between a behaviour and the arrival of a primary reinforcer as a consequence for desired behaviour. This combination of classical and operant conditioning allows the animal to observe the consequences of their behaviour and repeat those behaviours that are positively reinforced while the trainer shapes the animal's behaviour towards a final desired goal .

Clickers are not the only secondary reinforcer we could or do use. In place of the click we could substitute a whistle which is the secondary reinforcer that marine animal trainers use. Flags, a word, or a hand signal could also be used in place of the clicker. The fact that the clicker could be replaced by other secondary reinforcers emphasises the point that clickers are not magic. Whatever secondary reinforcer is used, the science is the same. Place a clicker in the stable and it does nothing, but pick it up, understand the science and have good hands, and the clicker has great possibilities. Always remember, training using a secondary reinforcer could just as easily be called whistle training or bridge training. That way we remember the skill is in the application of the science not in the tools we use.

CHAPTER 3

Where did clicker training come from?

One of the most common myths about clicker training is where it started. Most observers, books and websites incorrectly cite marine animal trainers as the founders of clicker training. Dolphin trainers did not actually create clicker training but these pioneers of scientific animal training do have to take credit for being the people who recognised the potential of operant conditioning and carried it on until it was used by Karen Pryor who, and then subsequently reintroduced it to the world in the early 1990s.

Delving a little deeper, a more interested student will soon discover that the scientist, B.F. Skinner was the first to describe the principles of operant conditioning on which clicker training is built. Skinner's work was built on the work of Edward L. Thorndike who developed the law of effect in 1911. However, B. F. Skinner was the first person to fully define operant conditioning in his 1938 book, *The Behaviour of Organisms*.

Skinner's work was based in the laboratory with pigeons and rats, and how his work made it into the practical world of animal training is a fascinating story. In 1938 Marian Kruse was Skinner's research assistant, helping him with his lab experiments. One day after being bitten by one of her rats Marian was on her way to get medical treatment when she literally bumped into Keller Breland. Keller was an ambitious and controversial psychology student. Through this chance meeting Keller was introduced to Skinner's work.

Marian and Keller were married in 1941 just as America entered the Second World War. Academic studies on hold, the Brelands joined Skinner in what was to be come known as Project Pelican. Skinner was sure that this new science of operant conditioning could be used to help the war effort and secured funds to develop the first guided bomb system. The system used three pigeons, strapped into the bomb. The pigeons were trained to peck at specific areas of a target image to guide the tail fins of the weapon. The loss of the pigeons was considered unfortunate but the potential for saving innocent human life was used to justify this.

Both Marian and Keller were extremely excited by this new science of animal training and were fascinated by operant conditioning, secondary reinforcers and schedules of reinforcement. They became determined to develop its practical application as soon as they could.

In 1943, Project Pelican was shelved and Marian and Keller bought a small farm and began to train a variety of animals. What was of most interest to the Brelands was the use of the secondary reinforcer. In Skinner's lab the pigeons had learned to associate the sounds of the feeder with the delivery of food. In fact, the sound of the feeder was used to shape the pigeons' behaviour. The Brelands saw the secondary reinforcer as a bridge between the reward and the behaviour. They developed the term "bridging stimulus" to describe the effect. Years later, dolphin trainers shortened this bridging stimulus to simply "bridge" and also applied the term to anything that created the secondary reinforcer such as whistles and clickers.

The Brelands experimented with toys, whistles and toy crickets to find the best secondary reinforcers, and they found the crickets were most suitable. With the use of the crickets and positive reinforcement the Brelands began to train a wide variety of animals.

The first domesticated animal to be "clicker trained" was the Breland's German shepherd dog named Gretel, thus disproving that clicker training started with dolphin trainers. At the Brelands' training farm, cats, goats, sheep, hamsters, raccoons, pigs and ducks soon followed Gretel, and in 1946 Marian even began to train chickens to be used to advertise farm animal feeds.

The 1950s saw Animal Behaviour Enterprises, as it was known by then, moved from Minnesota to Arkansas to a 245 acre farm. They produced several scientific dog training devices but unfortunately there was not much call for scientific dog training in the 1950s. It is a great pity that the opportunity was missed to advance dog training far beyond what was common place in the 1950s, as it would take another thirty years of punishment based training before the dog world would be ready to embrace the science of behaviour and positive reinforcement.

Animal Behaviour Enterprises grew and developed its role in advertising farm feeds. They trained all types of farm animals as well as salesmen to perform thousands of shows throughout America. Then the new media of television beckoned and Animal Behaviour Enterprises began to train animals for television commercials. Their shows and commercials included, dancing chickens, piano playing rabbits, chickens that chose the correct beer bottle, cows that unveiled the best feed and pigs that vacuumed and used scent discrimination to go shopping for the right products.

In 1951 Marian and Keller published a paper called "Applied Animal Psychology" which described how to use operant conditioning to train animals. After which, Skinner granted that Marian and Keller had founded the new field of Applied Animal Psychology. In his 1951 paper, "How to Teach Animals", Skinner described the use of a cricket (clicker) to train animals for the first time.

The television commercials continued into the 1960s and included cats and dogs as well as all the other animals they had been training. Animal Behaviour Enterprises was asked to develop parrot shows for Miami's Parrot Jungle and Marine Studios in Florida employed their skills. As a result of developing a dolphin act for Marine Studios, the Brelands published the first dolphin training manual.

As Marian and Keller became involved with training dolphins they met Bob Bailey who was a zoologist and the US Navy's Director of Training. Bailey worked with the Brelands to establish dolphin training programmes for the military. This is when secondary reinforcement training finally entered the mainstream marine animal training world. Bailey also developed an ambush detection system for the army using pigeons trained with operant conditioning.

Unfortunately, Keller Breland died in 1965 but Marian Breland and Bob Bailey continued with Animal Behaviour Enterprises and married in 1976. Together they worked on projects such as training pigeons to spot life rafts and life jackets at sea, enabling them to be spotters for coastguard rescue planes. Seagulls were trained to recover objects over huge distances, also to aid in rescue missions. Crows were trained to fly, guided by laser dots, to the windows of skyscrapers and use head mounted cameras to take pictures of the buildings' occupants. More than 140 species of animals and birds were trained by the Baileys, but Bob Bailey is probably best known for his work using a bridging stimulus to train dolphins.

B. F. Skinner is responsible for developing operant conditioning and Keller Breland, Marian Breland-Bailey and Bob Bailey are the pioneers who brought the practical application of the secondary reinforcer to the world. It is amazing to consider that the current clicker training revolution is really the second coming for the process. Nearly forty years before clicker training was reintroduced to the dog training world, the Brelands had already used it to train dogs, cats, chickens, rabbits, birds and farm animals of every description.

Many modern advocates of clicker training list the wide range of species that can now be trained using positive reinforcement with clicker training, not realising that these species had already been proved clicker trainable decades before.

Demonstrations of how animals can now be trained for television and films using only the positive reinforcement of clicker training forget to mention that forty five years ago it was already being done. The incredible ability of the clicker to train such a wide variety of new and imaginative behaviours is seen as a testament to the potential of clicker training and to the knowledge of modern trainers, rather than recognising that what the true pioneers did was even more amazing.

Given the climate and standard practices in animal training of the 1950s, the Brelands must have faced incredible opposition and scepticism for their methods and ideas. Sometimes modern trainers think it is hard to train and educate people in new and more ethical ways of training, but for the Brelands, just as for any pioneer, it must have been really difficult and very frustrating.

It is a great mystery to me why clicker training did not continue in the animal training world once the Brelands and Bob Bailey had been so successful using it.

But the marine animal world was ready. The Brelands' use of a conditioned reinforcer in dolphin training, and Bob Bailey's later use and avocation of a bridge, came at a time when captive dolphins were just beginning to appear beyond the military bases and research facilities. As captive dolphins became more common, training them and controlling them became essential, and so operant conditioning through the use of secondary reinforcers was in the right place at the right time. The bridging stimulus worked and it allowed the dolphins to earn their keep, entertaining the fee paying public, with fantastic shows based on the dolphin's natural behaviours. I always wonder if dolphins are really smarter than other species, or if, having been trained using positive reinforcement, they have simply been allowed to demonstrate their true potential. With the reintroduction of clicker training it seems that a lot of species are being allowed to demonstrate what they can really do. Following a workshop a few years ago, a participant who was using clicker training with dogs, but had not been around horses for ten years, concluded the workshop by asking, "When did horses get so smart?"

Perhaps clicker training did not catch on because other methods of training land animals worked and were, in general, acceptable to the public. Why change what was already working? In the 1940s and 1950s animals were not being credited with intelligence, let alone the ability to learn such complicated behaviour patterns and, therefore, clicker training obviously seemed surplus to requirements. Dolphins, however, are different. They are credited with being intelligent and talented at performing difficult feats of acrobatics and they are impossible to train using coercion. If you want to train dolphins you have to motivate them to work, or they swim off. This difference in the effectiveness of restraint between land animals and sea mammals is probably the reason clicker training persisted in the marine animal world and faded out in other species.

During the next twenty five years of dolphin training very little of the science of behaviour or clicker training seeped out for use in other species. However, during the 1980s some behaviourists were at least beginning to advocate non coercive behaviour based methods of training. Clicker training, as we know it today, really started in 1992 with a discussion at the Association for Behaviour Analysis meeting in San Francisco. A few days later, Karen Pryor, Gary Wilkes and Ingrid Shallenberger conducted a 'Don't Shoot the Dog' seminar attended by 250 dog trainers. Gary Wilkes had acquired some plastic clickers from a novelty shop and they proved to be excellent marker signals and teaching tools, that the seminar attendees took to them with enthusiasm. This seminar led to others, as well as to books and videos, and so clicker training was finally reborn in the dog world.

Since 1992 clicker training has spread into many spheres of animal training and husbandry. It is incredible to think we have had to wait nearly fifty years for the science of clicker training to come a full circle. Ok, in the 1940s it may not have been called clicker training and dolphin trainers may have used a whistle not a clicker to mark their trainees' behaviour, but the science and technology of clicker training has certainly been with us all this time. The small plastic and metal box has made the process of operant conditioning using secondary reinforcers more accessible to non-professional trainers and has produced to a less scientific and scary name for a scientific training method. However, it is important to remember that the clicker is a tool of the science not the science itself and, but for a novelty shop in 1992 selling clickers, we could just as easily had whistle training, bell training or even cricket training.

CHAPTER 4

What is the advantage of clicker training?

The most obvious advantage of using clicker training is the improvement in communication that can be achieved through the use of a bridging signal. However, there are a number of other side effects of using clicker training that a clicker trainer should be aware of in order to avoid problems by staying ahead of their equine student.

As seen in Chapter 2 the secondary reinforcer allows the trainer to bridge the gap in time between the required behaviour and the delivery of the primary reinforcer. One of the problems with equine clicker training equines compared to clicker training dogs is that in equines the trainer is often quite a way from the site of delivery of the reward, i.e. the mouth. As dogs are small, even when working at their rear end they are small enough for the trainer to only be an arm's length from the mouth. Also with a dog you can throw the reward and they may well catch it mid air. Throw a reward for a horse and it has to go look for it, further delaying the timing of the reward.

Trainers often say that for rewards or punishment to be effective they must reach the equine within three seconds of the behaviour they are meant to affect. If you actually count three seconds it is plenty long enough for the equine to have finished the relevant behaviour and be performing a completely different one when the reward arrives. A three second delay is far better than five seconds and near perfect compared to ten seconds, but the best connection between behaviour and reinforcer is the instant the behaviour happens. If the reward or punishment can be delivered at the moment the behaviour occurs, any vagueness in the message disappears.

A trainer simply provides information to the animal about what works and what does not. The animal has to figure out which behaviours elicit which responses. If the behaviour and the response are simultaneous then the animal's learning is made much easier and the number of repetitions required for the animal to make the connection will be dramatically reduced. It is this connection between a particular behaviour and the consistency of the response which determines the success of a trainer and the chosen training method. No matter what training method is being used, if the connection between the behaviour and response is very good, the training will work well. However, if the trainer has poor timing and is inconsistent with their communication this will create a poor connection between the target behaviour and the response, resulting in the animal's learning being dramatically slowed down.

When training a young horse to pick up their feet, there is a difficultly in giving the reward while the horse's foot is in the air. It is very difficult to get the timing right, given the trainer's distance from the animal's mouth and the fact that the trainer has their back to the horse's head and their hands full of hoof and leg. When the trainer gets the desired behaviour, such as the foot held calmly up, the trainer then has to put foot down, return to the head and offer the reward, by which time it is at least four to five seconds since the youngster had their foot in the air.

Once the equine is conditioned to the secondary reinforcer, in this case a clicker, the click is able to mark the required behaviour as the behaviour occurs. The animal can then connect the behaviour to the click and the positive reinforcement that the click has come to represent. For example, if we want to reward a mule for walking forward at our shoulder using rewards, this generally requires us to stop the animal to give it a scratch or food. The process of stopping interferes with the message the reward is supposed to deliver, but using clicker training a click can be given as the animal walks forward and is then stopped for a reward to be delivered. This way the animal receives the clearest information on the consequences of their behaviour. The faster and more accurate the information we can deliver the easier it will be for the equine to deliver the correct behaviour. Clicker training has the advantage of using a very unique sound that, when combined with the trainer's skill, can produce perfect timing in communication between the trainer and the horse, donkey or mule.

Of course you do not need to use a clicker to train these behaviours. By using negative reinforcement, positive reinforcement and punishment, a horse, donkey or mule can learn what is required of them but the advantage of the clicker is that it allows the animal to learn faster and without fear.

In the right hands the clicker can provide very accurate information about tiny behaviours that other methods of training struggle to identify. The possibility of perfect timing combined with a very short distinct sound means that another advantage of clicker training is the ability to mark very accurately only the required elements of a desired behaviour. To improve or change behaviour the trainer must select progressively more accurate examples of the final desired behaviour. Once the young horse has learnt to lift their leg up briefly, the trainer then has to communicate calmness, increased duration in the air and stillness of the foot if the behaviour is to be completed satisfactorily. The accuracy provided by the click means that even if the foot is only still for a couple of seconds that stillness can be marked very exactly. The foot can be lifted for increasing increments of time with each graduation carefully marked.

Any behaviour can be broken down to small achievable steps that can be added together to achieve the final behaviour. The smaller these chunks of information are, the easier it is for the animal to understand what is required. However, the smaller the step, the harder it is for the trainer to convey the message of which specific behaviour works to receive rewards. The accuracy in communication the clicker can provide overcomes this problem by giving the information and a powerful reward in a fraction of a second.

While running a workshop, a participant informed me that "the problem with clicker training is that your timing has to be so good." This is not the problem with clicker training. It is its strength. Whatever the chosen method of training, the trainer's timing should be as good as that required during clicker training. The difference with clicker training is that, because the timing is so accurately marked, we notice when the timing is poor. With other training methods poor timing is less noticeable especially when we are talking about just a second between good timing and bad.

The click can also mark the unwanted behaviours too but, because of the uniqueness of the sound and the ability to see timing, the trainer spots poor timing very quickly. With clicker training, if the click coincides with an undesired behaviour, the animal will quite likely offer that behaviour again. To the animal, the behaviour is not right or wrong but simply something that is rewarded or not. Fortunately, although they do happen, we do not need to worry about making mistakes as the process of clicker training is very forgiving. If we click the wrong behaviour and the animal offers it again, all we have to do is make sure we do not click that behaviour a second time and the behaviour will begin to die away, although the horse may offer it several times before they understand it does not work.

Clicker training has some other equally important advantages, such as using positive reinforcers to create operant conditioning. Both positive reinforcement and operant conditioning have an effect on the animal's learning. Scientifically speaking, operant conditioning relies on the animal to manipulate their own behaviour in order to change their environment and receive, remove or avoid the reinforcer.

Essentially, operant conditioning is a problem solving task. The animal must discover where reinforcements can be obtained and what is required to get it. How any animal goes about solving problems imposed on them depends on three factors:

- The evolutionary history of the species.
- The structure of the situation.
- The animal's past experiences of similar situations.

When faced with a problem, equines will first try those things that worked in similar situations in the past, either theirs or their ancestors. This is where a difficulty arises in all equine training. Equines are not naturally good problem solvers. Horses, donkeys and mules have good memories and can learn well but their evolution did not prepare them for complicated problem solving. If we consider predators such as cats and dogs, whose ancestors survived by being able to predict the complex behaviours of their prey, we can see why they have a reasonably good problem solving ability. In order to eat, the wolf had to work with and predict the behaviour of the pack, select the correct prey, predict their victim's behaviour and adapt accordingly. The reason equines do not have such a developed ability to solve problems is simply because grass never ran away from any equine!

This is not to say equines cannot solve problems or learn to solve problems. In the wild, problem solving is generally limited to either dealing with a situation or running away from it and, when they cannot run away, equines use their species specific defence reactions (SSDR) in an attempt to find a solution. Each species has a set of behaviours that they commonly use to deal with the problems they face. In equines their SSDR are to run, buck, rear, kick and bite.

Operant conditioning is an inference task where the individual's own behaviour is the best predictor of the reinforcer or reward. The animal's task is to figure out what behaviour precedes what reinforcer so that the next time they encounter that situation they can behave efficiently to gain the required reinforcer.

By using clicker training we expose the equine to operant conditioning and problem solving. The more problem solving the animal does, the better their problem solving skills become and the faster they learn to solve problems. Any form of training based on operant conditioning can improve on problem solving skills. However, clicker training has the advantage of using positive reinforcement which has even more added advantages.

Reinforcers are the goal or the motivator for the behaviour, but they also provide the feedback on the correctness of a given behaviour. Positive reinforcement tends to increase the range and numbers of behaviours being offered because the animal wants the consequences of their behaviour and does not fear making mistakes. Therefore, positive reinforcement is likely to increase the occurrence of all behaviours. For the trainer, more behaviours mean more opportunities to select the most appropriate behaviour to reward. This increased volume of accurate feedback increases the speed of learning as the animal has more information to learn from.

An advantage of a reward based system of training is that it causes the trainer to see the glass as half full. If we are looking for behaviour to reward we tend to see a more positive side to an animal's action or reactions. This positive attitude has a good effect on the relationship between the human and equine. The increase in positive association to the trainer builds trust and increases motivation to work with the trainer. As animals become less fearful of the consequences of their behaviour they offer more behaviour and initially receive more rewards.

There is a common belief that you should never train an equine in their living environment, such as their field or stable, as they could associate the area with the unpleasant consequences of work and then be unable to relax in these areas.

This saying is probably true if the training is based on negative reinforcement and punishment. The positive nature of clicker training means, if it is used as I set out later in this book, it is perfectly acceptable to use it in the animal's stable or field. In fact, good clicker training is very good for equines on box rest, helping to provide mental stimulation and alleviate boredom. Some horses that have been clicker trained during box rest have been reported to finish box rest calmer and further on in their training than when the box rest started.

Another advantage of clicker training is that the trainer can see the accuracy of their timing. While using a clicker it is easy to see the behaviour you wish to mark and hear the click at the same time. It is as if the sense of sight and sound overlay each other and the trainer is able to observe the accuracy of the click. It is common to hear clicker trainer draw breath and say "missed it" or "that click was late". This observable timing helps to provide feedback to the trainer about their own skill and, if required, encourages them to practise their timing.

Using clicker training can improve the trainer's ability to shape behaviour and plan ahead. As the animal makes progress in their learning the trainer needs to be able to identify very small elements of required behaviours in order to reinforce them. This means that the clicker trainer should plan ahead and prepare for the lesson in advance. Good clicker trainers tend to have written shaping plans for their lessons as the horse is learning so fast it is often difficult to keep up. Without knowing where you are going in a lesson there is little hope of getting there by the most direct route.

One of the advantages of using clicker training with any species is how well lessons and the concept of clicker training are retained. On two occasions, in my early days of clicker training, I trained horses to pick up a small plastic cone and pass the cone to me. Both were new to clicker training, one was a fourteen year-old stock horse in Australia, and the other a seven year-old pony in Holland. Having taught these behaviours and completed my other work abroad I returned to the

UK. In each situation I returned to both animals four months later. Once I was back with these animals I was tempted to see just how much they remembered. With no clicker training between my visits I thought perhaps they would nudge the cone, maybe even try to pick it up, drop it and then search for the reward. However, on both occasions they looked at me, looked at the cone, reached down picked it up and very carefully passed it to me. Perhaps because of the positive nature of clicker training or the lack or worry about the consequences of their behaviour both animals had perfectly retained this novel behaviour.

To demonstrate the ability of clicker training to make lessons stick, I even have a clicker-trained goldfish. I trained my fantail goldfish called Karen to touch a target and to swim through a hoop suspended in the tank. I could not use a clicker as the sound would not carry underwater so I tapped the surface of the water as a bridge between the behaviour and food. Having trained this behaviour I tested Karen's memory by not working with her for three weeks. I thought this was a long time given their supposed three second memory. When I reintroduced the hoop, after a brief pause, she offered the required behaviours. After this I did not show her the hoop for eighteen months. Even after that length of time, when I returned the hoop to the tank, within a few minutes and a few rewards, Karen swam through it. So much for a three-second memory.

There are many stories of horses remembering clicker lessons months and even years later. Often when a clicker trained horse has a problem with something, even if months have passed since the last clicker lesson, the trainer will reach for the clicker. The horse immediately understands the click and starts working to receive rewards, thereby dealing with the problem faced. It seems that the positive nature of clicker training and the clarity of communication really help animals to remember what is required and to be motivated enough to offer behaviours that might be rewarded even months later.

Clicker training also promotes thinking in the equine, develops problem-solving skills whilst improving the relationship with the trainer and increasing the trainer's skill levels. It is no wonder that clicker training sounds like a perfect solution to equine training problems. Unfortunately, there are some possible consequences of these advantages in equine learning. If you want your horse, donkey or mule to be a willing partner to whom you are prepared to listen, even if they disagree with your decisions sometimes then clicker training might be for you. If you want an animal who can solve problems, even ones you do not want solved, then clicker training could help achieve these goals.

However, if you do not want an equine that really thinks, do not start clicker training. Most people believe that they want their equine to think more, that it will be fantastic to have an equine partner that can solve problems and is fast at learning, but if you start clicker training you will need to be ready for the additional problems this method can bring.

A clicker-trained horse could well start to offer behaviours, and lots of them, in the hope of receiving a reward. They may offer behaviours when you do not want them to. Many trainers have regretted teaching their horse to play football or Spanish walk as, when offering such behaviours to solve a problem, the animal has kicked the trainer in the kneecap. The more behaviours that are offered, the more concentration the trainer must have to deal with all this new activity. The animal can literally bombard the trainer with behaviours in the hope of getting the reward and then it becomes difficult for the animal to concentrate on what the trainer really requires.

Equines that learn to solve problems do not always solve the problems they face in the way the trainer wants. They begin to try new solutions to old problems and again the trainer has to be ready for this change in behaviour. As the animal becomes more confident they may challenge the trainer's leadership and decisions. If the animal does not fear the consequences of their actions because they have become overly confident through the use of clicker training they may do things they would not normally do, such as pull faces, threaten to kick or nip. This change in behaviour can be temporary but if the trainer is not prepared for it and accidentally rewards it, this new behaviour can be effective for the animal, thereby making it more permanent.

Many clicker trained equines show signs of frustration when the reward is withheld or removed completely and this frustration at failing to receive a reward can cause aggressive responses. However, as you will learn in later chapters, this frustration can be reduced if clicker training is introduced in an equine specific way.

The most damaging consequences of clicker training to the animal is when the animal learns to think and solve problems using positive reinforcement but the owner becomes frustrated or even angry at the animal's change in behaviour and smacks or punishes the behaviour. This single act of punishment can damage the trust the animal has in the trainer and cause the equine to develop an emotional conflict between wanting the rewards of clicker training but fearing that it might receive punishment instead. Equines do not deal well with this sort of conflict and it can lead to fear, frustration and stress.

Although very little scientific evidence exists on the effectiveness of equine clicker training, and that which does has not found an improvement of learning speed or retention, it is to me common sense that if the trainer can provide an increased level of accurate information on which behaviours are effective then the animal's learning will become faster.

Perhaps because trainers have been clicker training equines the same way dogs are clicker trained, to clicker training in equines has not yet reaching its potential as a teaching tool.

All in all, clicker training has fantastic advantages but there are also some potential problems that can occur in some horses and, because of their size, these problems can be very serious. Luckily, if we begin our clicker training correctly and understand the differences between clicker training equines and other species, many of these potential problems can be avoided. I would urge any potential clicker trainer to consider the possible side effects and if they have any doubts in their mind about their ability to deal with these problems to get further training and good professional advice and plenty of practice before they start clicker training their horses.

CHAPTER 5

Is clicker training for equines just like clicker training dogs?

As we have seen, clicker training started with dogs, was then used with dolphins and returned to dogs before arriving in the equine world without much change in the method of application between the species. Therefore, the clicker training of equines has been done in the same way that the clicker training of dogs is done or for that matter in the same way dolphins are clicker-trained. However, there is a growing awareness among people who are using clicker training that perhaps there may be some very important differences between these species when it comes to learning and using clicker training.

The real answer to the question, "Is clicker training equines the same as clicker training dolphins and dogs?" is, of course, yes and no. Regardless of the species the use of the clicker as a conditioned reinforcer is governed by the science of behaviour. Whether we are clicker training a dog or a donkey the clicker is used as a bridge between the required behaviour and the arrival of a primary reinforcer. The rules that govern positive reinforcement and the use of operant conditioning are also the same in different species. So the science of clicker training and the principles of behaviour are the same for dogs and equines.

Unfortunately, the replication of scientific principles is where the similarities between training equines and canines stop. It is probably the most obvious thing in the world to say, but dolphins are not dogs and dogs are not donkeys. So why would we think that their training would be the same? While the science of clicker training is the same, the mechanics of application is different between species. As an example, the most obvious species difference is the fact you cannot motivate a dog to work using a handful of grass as a reward or the fact that horses do not work for tennis balls, but the differences do go much deeper than this.

Currently, most trainers who use clicker training for horses do, in fact, apply the same rules as they would for clicker training dogs. That is just the way that clicker training has evolved. However, over my ten years of clicker training equines, I have noticed some important behavioural differences between species and I have some very good reasons I do not clicker train horses, donkeys and mules the same way as dogs.

The difference between the evolution of equines and canines has left us with very different animal, not just in the way they look or feed but in the way they think, how they are motivated and how they interact with humans.

Dogs evolved from social pack animals that cooperated to hunt their prey and in doing so had to solve problems. The modern dogs' ancestors had to hunt to survive and consequently dogs are very willing and usually highly motivated to work for food rewards. Mistakes made out hunting meant the pack might go hungry until more prey could be located. Most hunts end in failure and so reaction to failure is to continue hunting. This natural persistence helps dogs to keep trying to get their rewards.

Equines, on the other hand, evolved in social herds where cooperation generally only extended to an understanding that there is a safety in numbers. Equine food sources may at times be sparse and separated by considerable distances but they never run away, hide or try to escape. Horses do not have to creep up on a blade of grass. As a result of their feeding strategies, equines have not developed the innate problem solving skills that we see in dogs. As an example of the differences between species, dogs can be quite successful at maze tasks, while horses show less innate ability with the same challenges.

Mistakes in the equine herd, especially when avoiding predators, could be fatal and so it seems to me that equines have evolved with a lower tolerance to failure. In experiments, when horses are faced with making a choice between two behaviours, with the wrong one resulting in punishment – although through learning they will make fewer mistakes – they will be slower to take the decision about which behaviour to perform. The evolutionary differences also mean that horses tend to need more time to make decisions in the early stages of clicker training. Depending on their individual distinctiveness, it is not unusual for a horse, to take ten to fifteen seconds before offering a behaviour. Dogs on the other hand tend, in general, to offer lots of responses and often seem to need less time to offer behaviours.

Horses naturally have a lower motivation for working for food rewards as it is not something their ancestors have had to become efficient at. This is, fortunately, compensated for to a large degree by the fact that in domestication food variety is limited, so novel or high value foods can be very motivating for equines but less so than for dogs.

Experiments in learning also confirm that different species perform better when their predominant sense is used. Rats perform badly in visual discrimination tests but very well in smell discrimination tests. Rats have poor eye sight and a great sense of smell. Equines have been shown to be better at problem-solving where direct visual solutions are available. Added to this complex mix of learning ability is the difference in individual performance due to either genetics and/or previous experience and we have the clearest indication of the differences between equine learning and learning in dogs or dolphins.

The differences demonstrated in equine learning and problem solving lead me to ensure that equines are always allowed plenty of time to learn how clicker training works. It is also crucially important to develop an individual's problem solving skills before moving on to more challenging behaviours or problems. For most equines, having to touch a target held at arm's length from a bum bag full of food in order to get that food initially makes no sense. Equines are used to going directly to what they want to eat, putting their heads down and eating. This direct to source behaviour is why it is so important to teach equines not to mug for food during the first few training sessions. Learning to learn and developing problem-solving abilities are essential elements that must be included at the start of the clicker training process in equines.

Horses have a tendency to mug for food because it makes sense for them. This, added to the fact that they are much bigger and heavier than dogs, immediately adds a safety concern to training equines which does not exist for canine training. In some cases, it may be necessary, for safety, to start clicker training a horse from behind the stable door or over a stable door chain until they understand the rules and boundaries of clicker training. In some cases it may be best to work with the horse without clicker training to establish good safe handling behaviour, before beginning clicker training. A horse mugging for treats can be dangerous and through training the equine needs to learn that mugging does not work. These lessons must be incorporated into early training sessions with all equines with whom food rewards will be used.

The nature of our social interaction with equines and canines also creates differences in training. Our family dog spends considerable more time with us in our environment than a horse, donkey or mule does. With a dog we may have a clicker training session for a few minutes and then spend the next five or six hours together in the house before we have another clicker training session. Equines, on the other hand, tend to see us for relatively short lengths of time before being left again to their own devices for the next twelve hours. This limited time together can lead to problems if the trainer, clicker trains the horse every time they visit. Pretty soon, the horse associates food with the trainer and expects food rewards to be available whenever the trainer is present and this can lead to mugging and frustration for both trainer and horse. When we clicker train equines, early training sessions must include lessons about identifying when clicker training is available and when it is not. Dogs also learn these signs, although they are not deliberately taught, because they spend so much time with us not clicker training they have more information to identify the differences.

Equines are flight animals who are easily scared by novel items and yet much of what we want them to learn revolves around learning to deal with scary situations and objects. Clicker training equines often involves teaching the animal to overcome their fears and phobias. The reaction to these fears can be big and dangerous. A 500 kilogramme horse trying to avoid what they perceive as a threatening situation is considerably more dangerous than a dog in the same position. To prevent accidents during training we have to shape behaviour more effectively and stretch comfort zones more gradually with equines, because there is a greater chance of serious injury than with dogs.

Many of the behaviours we teach horses are considerably different from those we teach dogs. There is a need with equines to teach them duration behaviours such as holding their feet up for longer, walking further, standing still for longer under increasing exposure to a scary object. While we can teach dogs similar behaviours often we want them to perform behaviours that have a natural conclusion such as sit, fetch, roll over and come.

One of the problems that equine clicker trainers notice is the difficulty in extending duration behaviours when the click normally ends the animal's behaviour. Using dog training methods, as soon as the click occurs, the animal stops the behaviour in order to look for the reward. This is not great if we want to get horses to hold up their feet for longer, because as soon as they hear the click they snatch back their foot and turn around looking for a reward. To overcome this problem, we have to use a system where we can provide a keep-going signal as well as a terminal bridge that ends the behaviour. These two pieces of information make it easier to extend behaviours. It is also extremely important to teach patience from the start of clicker training sessions. Using normal clicker training for dogs, equines can become frustrated if their reward is delayed or if the rewards are withheld in order to increase the behaviour or to put the behaviour on a variable schedule of reinforcement. A frustrated or impatient horse can cause injury to humans or itself. By specifically teaching patience in early sessions of clicker training, frustration is minimised and the removal of the clicker from training is made easier and safer.

There are also a host of minor fundamental differences in training equines and dogs. Dogs do not take long to consume rewards – a couple of seconds and the reward is gone and the dog is looking for the next one. For an equine, a piece of carrot can take ten to twenty seconds to chew and swallow, thereby slowing the whole process of clicker training.

We can substitute play and toys as a reward for dogs but equines do not tend to see fetching a ball as a reward for work. Equally, we can use scratches or mutual grooming as a replacement for food rewards in some equines but this is not something that is deliberately done in clicker training dogs because they work so well for food and toys and with very few of the unwanted side effects these reinforcers can produce in equines.

It is obvious there are a number of differences between the behaviour and learning of equines and other species and most training methods take account of these differences. While natural horsemanship has become popular with equines we do not hear much talk of natural dolphinmanship, where the trainer tries to act like another dolphin in order to create a bond and get the animal to perform. Using punishment with killer whales is inadvisable and ineffective, but many horse trainers often resort to whips, spurs and bigger bits to solve a horse problem. Putting a choke chain on a dolphin or even on a cat would be ineffective, yet their use is common in dog training.

We already recognise the differences in training different species. As far as I know there is no other method of training dogs that is applied in the same way for horses, yet for some reason the procedure of clicker training dogs seems to have been applied directly to equines without much modification. Perhaps this is why there have been mixed results for clicker training equines and limitations and problems have appeared that have not existed in dogs.

If we make some changes to the mechanics of clicker training we can accommodate the differences in species specific behaviour between dogs and equines. These changes in process increase the safety and effectiveness of clicker training equines, while minimising unwanted side-effects such as mugging and frustration.

Perhaps in the excitement of using this new method and with the potential power of positive reinforcement, trainers just got straight on with training and in their enthusiasm to use something other than punishment and negative reinforcement they forgot equines are not dolphins or dogs.

It is the time for equine clicker training to evolve in order to accommodate the species differences and, as we progress through the process of teaching clicker training, I will highlight the new adaptations for equine specific clicker training.

So the alternative answer to our original question of whether clicker training equines is just like clicker training dogs is that, currently, it is not different, but it should be!

CHAPTER 6

Doesn't using food rewards cause equines to bite?

Throughout the history of equine domestication there has been a common belief that feeding equines by hand to causes them to bite. Therefore, it is only natural that this belief continues to be one of the main obstacles and objections to clicker training. Indeed, anyone who has been around horses or donkeys for any length of time will have seen examples of them mugging well intentioned owners for sugar lumps or pieces of carrot. Having seen this behaviour it is easy to draw the conclusion that any sort of hand feeding is likely to cause equines to bite. However, my experience has been that if food rewards are used correctly they do not teach horses, donkeys or mules to bite nor do they have to lead to mugging behaviour. Unfortunately, just like every other element of equine training, only the correct use of food as a reward avoids unwanted behaviour.

If food is used incorrectly, the notion that it causes equines to bite appears true. However, if we consider that all equines have their feed restricted by domestication and are given feed by humans, yet not all equines bite we begin to see that food itself cannot be the cause of biting or food aggression. The factor influencing the behaviour of the animal is the timing, knowledge and consistency of the trainer and this has more influence over equine behaviour than the food alone. Food does not cause equines to bite, however, the poor timing and delivery of the food can do. To understand how food might cause an equine to bite we need to establish the science behind how equines learn to obtain food from humans.

Ancestors of modern equines had only to find food, and if they could see and reach it first they could eat it. Throughout their evolution, equines have always gone directly to the food that they can see or smell in order to obtain that food. Unlike dogs that have evolved to hunt and chase food, it initially makes no sense to an equine to do something completely unrelated in order to get food they can smell in a trainer's pocket. Consequently, when a horse smells food in a pocket or bum bag their first reaction is go straight to the location of the food and to explore the area and, if possible, obtain some food. This is normal behaviour for equines and makes perfect sense to them.

If we return to the science of positive reinforcement we see that positive consequences that follow an action are likely to increase the chances of that behaviour happening again. Through this simple process equines for generations have been learning to mug humans for food rewards. If their exploration of the food containing area should be successful, either accidentally or through poor timing of the trainer, then the behaviour which the animal believes immediately preceded the arrival of food is likely to be repeated. Through this accidental reinforcement the horse, donkey or mule begins to learn that exploring the food area may well bring access to the food. But this is only the first part of the story.

Once the animals have learnt how to obtain food from the "human vending machine" they will try to get food whenever they can, especially if their motivation for the novel food is particularly high. If the trainer always gives food on minimal demand, biting behaviour is unlikely to develop. The animal may demand food by continually exploring the food area but it will not need to do any more than that to receive the food. At this point it is important to remember that the animal is not aware of right or wrong behaviour, only of behaviour that is effective in getting rewards and those behaviours which are not.

The real problems begin when, for whatever reason, the trainer withholds the food from the exploring animal. Here the science of behaviour can explain what happens next. Behaviour that has previously been effective at producing a reward is more resistant to extinction. This resistance means that when an effective behaviour suddenly fails to work, the animal will repeat the behaviour, sometimes very vigorously, in what is called an extinction burst. For example, if a we put money into a vending machine hoping to receive a bar of chocolate in exchange for pushing the correct buttons and the chocolate bar fails to arrive, the first action we will normally try is to push the buttons again, faster and then with more force, hoping that the machine will start releasing chocolate. This increase in button pushing is an extinction burst.

If button pushing fails to deliver the chocolate the human may be tempted to shake or even kick the vending machine in an attempt to get the reward. How determined the human is to get chocolate will depend on the individual's need for chocolate at the moment. The higher the motivation, the more vigorous the assault on the vending machine may be. If, just after it is kicked, the vending machine delivers the chocolate the human is likely to come to the belief that reluctant vending machines are best trained by kicking them.

Let's return to the horse that has learnt to mug the trainer in order to get food. When the food suddenly stops arriving, the mugging behaviour is likely to increase in speed and strength and in the case of a highly food motivated equine, it may increase even to include a nip. If at any point during this extinction burst the animal receives food either accidentally or it is given intentionally by the unaware trainer, then this new more vigorous mugging and or biting behaviour will be reinforced and, therefore, it is likely to be repeated. This is how food rewards teach equines to bite and mug for food. Unintentionally, generations of well meaning owners and trainers have given equines a reputation for mugging and biting wher-ever food is involved, not realising it is their own behaviour that was causing the animal to bite.

What is clear is that food does not cause equines to bite but the timing of the arrival of food does. To avoid learning to bite to receive food, equines have to learn an unnatural way of behaving around food. They have to learn new 'safer' behav-iours that will be successful in bringing food rewards. Fortunately, equines are quick learners and can, if provided with the correct information, very happily learn how to get food without mugging

It has been my experience that equines can receive food rewards and still be perfectly well mannered and safe. This happens only if the animal is allowed to learn two things. Firstly, the animal must learn that mugging behaviour is unsuccessful at getting food rewards. Secondly, the animal must learn which behaviours are followed by food rewards. These two separate pieces of learning can then work together to ensure that mugging behaviour is avoided when using food as a reward.

The first part of using food rewards in my experience is to always use a bum bag, treat pouch or waistcoat, that is only used for food work. Two things happen when we adopt this approach: our pockets, stop smelling of food so the animal stops searching for food rewards in our pockets and the animal becomes clearly aware of when food rewards are avail-able and even more importantly when they are not. In effect the bum bag becomes a "clicker training is available" signal. With this signal in place the horse quickly learns that food is only available when the bum bag or waistcoat is on and this prevents the animal from constantly searching for food during every interaction. This clear signal also means that the animal learns not to continually offer all their trained behaviours during every human interaction in hope of being rewarded.

To understand this signal the animal has to be taught about the meaning of the bum bag or treat pouch etc. For the first five to ten lessons the bum bag should be used and then at the end of the session, the bag taken off and removed from the training area. Then the trainer should return to the equine and spend a few minutes of quality time just being with the animal. This gives the horse, donkey or mule the chance to explore the possibility of receiving food when the bum bag is not present and after several sessions the animal will learn that food is only available when the bag is present and therefore food rewards are not available at any other time.

When the bum bag is on and has rewards in it, the superb equine sense of smell will soon locate the source of food and, as I have already said, it is natural for an equine to go straight to the food and try and get some. At this point the animal should be allowed to carefully explore the trainer and bum bag. However, great care should be taken to ensure that they cannot get any food rewards. Again this exploring behaviour has to happen in order for the animal to learn that mugging behaviour does not result in food.

A common mistake for trainers is not allowing the animal to explore the bum bag for fear they will learn to mug. Because we do not want the animal to mug we do not allow them to explore to see if mugging works. In order to learn that food rewards can only be gained when the bum bag is present but that food cannot be directly accessed from the bum bag the horse has to explore the possibilities. If the animal is prevented from exploring mugging behaviour then they are unable to discover that mugging is ineffective at receiving rewards. Mugging will only work if the animal is rewarded for it in someway.

When working with an equine that has shown food aggressive tendencies, extra care must be taken to avoid personal injury. This may mean that the food aggression must be worked with first and removed before clicker training is introduced. In less established cases, or where the animal has previously learnt to mug due to poor trainer timing, the horse may be best worked with over a stable door or stall chain that provides an extra element of safety until the animal has leant that mugging behaviour is no longer effective. In either case, only a fully competent trainer should train equines that are food aggressive or mug for food

Having taught the animal what does not work, we must then teach them what will be successful in securing food rewards from the trainer. In effect we are training an incompatible behaviour. If the animal is taught that standing still with their head forward brings rewards then they are likely to do this in preference to mugging behaviour.

There are two ways of training a more suitable behaviour, one is to wait until the animal has their head straight forward away from the trainer and to click and reward. Provided that clicks and food rewards only arrive when the animal's head is forward or away from the trainer they will soon learn only this behaviour gets rewards. They will be less able to mug if their head has to be kept away from the trainer in order to receive reward. The second way to teach an incompatible behaviour is using a target. The target can be just about anything that is easy to handle and easy for the animal to see. Purpose designed targets with handles are good because they give the trainer scope to position the target at greater distances from their body as training progresses.

The final element in avoiding mugging behaviour in clicker trained equines is to teach the animal patience from the first lesson. Many clicker trainers have found difficulties with their animals snatching for food once the click is heard. It can also be quite common for the animal to be frustrated when the trainer tries to withhold the click in order to extend the duration of the desired behaviour. To solve this I have adapted the science of behaviour to suit clicker training equines which, as we have seen, should be different from clicker training dogs. Teaching patience begins by withholding the food reward for three to four seconds after the click as this teaches the animal to wait and not just snatch for the reward as soon as they hear the click. Withholding the reward also starts the process of fading out the use of the click. By withholding the food after the click the equine learns to wait and this patience in waiting for the reward can then be used to increase the duration of the behaviour by adding in intermediate and terminal bridges. Teaching patience at a very early stage allows the click to be faded out much more easily and with less frustration than has been previously possible. More detail on this process can be found in the chapter on getting started.

Using these methods, we can easily teach equines that mugging behaviour does not work and that other behaviours are more successful at gaining rewards. However, the key to success is to remember that the process needs to be learnt and that to learn the animal will need to make a few mistakes. It is natural for them to attempt to mug, but it is very important they explore this behaviour, if they need to, in order to gain an understanding that mugging does not work.

The use of food as a reward during equine training will only cause equines to bite if biting behaviour is effective at receiving rewards. It really is that simple. Due to their nature, equines will search for food where they smell it or see it and must learn which more suitable domesticated behaviours are effective at getting food rewards. Food does not cause equines to bite but poor timing and a lack of understanding of the learning process by the trainer does.

CHAPTER 7

Can anyone do it and with every equine?

Clicker training has been portrayed in many equine magazines as the ultimate solution in equine training, capable of dealing with all problems. The positive nature of the training and the enthusiasm that it generates in most equines creates an image of happiness, fun and success not found in most other training methods. Clicker training appeals to people who want a truly positive relationship with their equine, and to those who want to feel that the animal chooses to work with them, as opposed to having to work for them. Clicker training does indeed have a great deal of potential to enhance the human equine relationship. However, despite all the hype, promise and positive nature of clicker training, just like other methods of equine training it has its limitations.

There are two things to assess when considering the suitability of clicker training for everyone and all situations; first, the horse, donkey or mule and, second, the trainer. The clicker is a plastic and metal box; it is a tool or an aid to training, much like a head collar, pressure halter, whip or bit. Just like these other training aids the clicker's success or failure is in the hands of the trainer. Regardless of whether the trainer is any good, the use of any aid will create some form of learning for the animal. The quality and success of the learning will depend on the trainer's ability and the equine's individual nature.

As with all learning and training, there will be occasions

when despite a less than suitable situation, success has been created, usually by the skill, timing and patience of the trainer and the learning ability of the equine. So, rather than stating clicker training should never be used with a certain type of horse or trainer, I really want to highlight where extreme care should be taken and when less experienced trainers should give very careful consideration before choosing to continue.

We will start by looking at situations where limitation may be created by the equines individual nature.

Equine limitation number 1

The horse, donkey or mule that is extremely nervous of humans may not initially be the most suitable candidate for clicker training. While clicker training using food can help to create a positive association of the human to food, it is not always the ideal way to build a trusting relationship. A nervous animal that is fearful of humans will want to run away from perceived danger. If the animal is also motivated by food a conflict can arise, pitting the fear of humans against the desire for food. Equines in general are not good at dealing with decisions created between two equal, conflicting choices.

I have found the horse that is truly convinced of the untrustworthy nature of humans, through past experiences, will not even want to overcome this fear for any type of reward. An extremely nervous equine may even panic at the sound of the click and have to get used to the noise before they can progress. The nervous animal may not want to take food from the trainer's hand, which further complicates the training.

If the animal's motivation for food proves greater than the fear of the human, they will learn to approach the food source. However, the animal's approach can mask the animal's underlying fear and if their approach is mistaken for a lack of fear the animal can be put in a situation where they are overexposed to a fearful stimulus and their flight mechanism is engaged and, this can lead to injury to animal or human.

When working with a nervous animal I believe training is about developing trust and learning about each other in order to understand what the animal requires and what their true nature may be. Perhaps it would be best to consider this situation in human terms. If we were shy and nervous, perhaps we had even had a bad experience previously with people and then a stranger turns up and starts to give us £1 coins just for being near them, how would our relationship look? The stranger does not say much but continues to give us £1 coins as long as we are near them. We want the money but what are we learning about this stranger? We are getting richer, but are we really getting to know and trust this person? If their behaviour changes and they start to invade our personal space, at what point is their behaviour no longer worth accepting the £1? I believe equines need to learn to trust humans and that the best relationships are ones started on solid foundations of acceptance and knowledge usually achieved through the use of body language.

Trainers tend to use clicker training with nervous animals as a way of counter conditioning, which means pairing something good like food with something the animal perceives as negative, in this case the human, so the negative will take on a positive association. Training a nervous animal is not just about being patient or nice to the animal through the use of positive reinforcement. Successful training requires the animal to expand their comfort zones to humans and being handled. The horse, donkey or mule needs to be gently stretched mentally and physically in order to reach their potential. If the animal receives food for just being near the human the animal's comfort zones are kept limited. Once the trainer wants more commitment from the animal, or for them to accept being handled, the animal's comfort zones can be massively over reached and problems occur.

With nervous horses I like to get to know them a little first, be around them, build trust so that, even without rewards, I let them learn I am not going to cause them pain, or make sudden movements to trap them. In some situations a good trainer could use clicker training to get a nervous horse to come up and accept being touched but there is then a doubt in the trainer's mind. Does this horse want to be touched or does it just want carrots? As long as we recognise this possible conflict, we can use clicker training.

Wherever possible I like to work on building a relationship first with as few pieces of equipment as possible and then to introduce clicker training after gaining the animal's trust and learning about the animal's character without the distractions of food.

Equine limitation number 2

Whenever we are working with an equine behavioural problem, pain should be the first possibility that we eliminate as a cause of unwanted behaviour. Many equine problems are caused by pain created either through injury or through the use of poorly maintained or ill-fitting tack. Clicker training can be highly motivating to an animal and can cause them to work even though they are in pain. If this happens, pain and pleasure are like a balance scale. If the pain is small and the motivation for food high the animal will continue to work for the rewards, perhaps aggravating a minor injury or masking its existence altogether. This masking can be quite common with feet problems, such as kicking or reluctance to lift or hold the feet up. If the pain is larger than the pleasure gained from the rewards then the motivation to work will be greatly reduced and possibly the animal will link the clicker training to pain.

It is all too easy for the inexperienced trainer to reach for the "magic clicker" without fully investigating the causes of the problem. Changes in behaviour or behaviours that are not in keeping with the animal's normal character should be fully investigated by a vet or suitably qualified equine professional before clicker training is commenced. Pain needs to be alleviated before clicker training is commenced.

Of course there are always exceptions to the pain rule and I have been in situations where I have used clicker training to help animals that have injured themselves and are reluctant to have the area touched for treatment. In these situations I used short one off sessions to allow the animal to receive the immediate treatment that they required. I do not go straight to the injury and expect the animal to stand still for the occasional reward while they are pain. I do not train the animal to perform a task or behaviour other than standing still. I shape the behaviour with small steps that are the least uncomfortable for the animal so the pain and pleasure balance is maintained. In most cases the clicker can be removed rapidly and is replaced with counter conditioning between the treatment and food rewards alone.

Equine limitation number 3

In the previous chapter, we looked at the importance of the correct use and timing of food rewards and considered the use of food rewards with food aggressive animals. Food aggression is a term used to label equines that show aggressive behaviour in proximity to food. This behaviour can develop from a number of causes which include previous deprivation of food and excessive competition for food within a herd environment. Food aggression can even be a learnt behaviour. Whatever the cause, the food aggressive animal uses aggressive signals or actual aggression to increase the chances of getting food.

If an equine has shown aggressive tendencies around food then the introduction of clicker training using food can be dangerous. If the animal believes aggression increases the chances of getting food that will be their first choice of behaviour for obtaining food during clicker training. This increases the risk of injury to the trainer and of the horse being further reinforced for aggressive behaviour.

In order to use clicker training with this type of behaviour the equine must first learn that aggressive behaviour is not rewarded with food. This can be done but, is of course, a potentially dangerous piece of work and should be carried out by experienced trainers. Even with an experienced trainer, the clicker training process should be started with the animal safely contained, usually behind a stable door or stable chain.

I personally prefer not to start food aggressive animals with clicker training but use operant conditioning and systematic desensitization to alleviate the problem. Essentially, this requires teaching the horse patience and that other more suitable behaviour is more successful at acquiring rewards.

It is possible to use scratches as the reward in place of food for food aggressive equines. The animal has to perceive scratches as a reward and their motivation for scratches can change at different times of year depending on the state of their coat or the sensitivity of their skin.

Equine limitation number 4

The equine's ability to work with clicker training is really dependent on their initial ability to solve problems and offer behaviour for which they can be rewarded. Animals that have experienced excessive punishment during training or aggressive negative reinforcement are less likely to offer behaviours or try to do so because their previous experience has not encouraged them to solve problems and has conditioned them to fear the consequences of their actions. An equine that has come from such a negative environment may initially be uninterested or limited in their ability to work with clicker training.

On one workshop, I worked with a Welsh Cob mare named Poppy, who belonged to the owners of a large equine facility. They were not attending the workshop but offered Poppy to me to help demonstrate clicker training. As they handed

Poppy over to me they informed me that she was being trained to drive but was stubborn and wilful as well as prone to panicking and that she needed a lot of the use of the whip to make her do anything.

As I started introducing the clicker, Poppy did indeed seem stubborn and wilful. She was hardly interested in her surroundings and had no interest in working with me. After a couple of free food rewards her motivation was slightly raised so I offered her the target to touch. Even though it was right in front of her she stood for fifteen seconds before reaching to explore it. During our short training session Poppy continued to work extremely carefully she only made one mistake during the session but took ten to fifteen seconds every time before committing to action. It was clear Poppy had never been taught to solve problems and that she feared the consequences of her behaviour. Far from being wilful and stubborn, Poppy was actually extremely cautious and fearful.

Although clicker training will help a horse like Poppy it takes more patience than normal and a greater understanding of the processes of behaviour. I feel that horses, donkeys or mules that have come from negative environments or negative training methods need time to adjust and relax before commencing clicker training.

Once introduced to positive reinforcement and clicker training it would be perfectly normal for equines that have previously been mistreated to test the boundaries of their new-found freedom. To learn their new boundaries the animal must push the trainer and the environment to discover what is acceptable and what is not. This can mean the animal may offer a threat bite or kick. They may barge a little or pull on the lead. During this process of learning, consistency and persistence are vital to establish safe behaviour without crushing the animals desire to learn. When using clicker training in these situations it can be difficult to establish boundaries in behaviour, as other behaviours, such as dragging the handler to grass, are self-rewarding, so the motivation to work for the reward or click are lost. I again find it is often advantageous to work with the animal to establish the behaviours that are required for safe domestication using as few tools as possible and, once the relationship is formed and the rules established, then clicker training can be introduced.

Equine limitation number 5

Positive reinforcement creates a thinking equine that learns to solve problems. At first this does not seem to be a reason to avoid clicker training. After all, this is one of its main benefits. However, not everyone is ready to have an equine that thinks and offers lots of behaviours in the hope of receiving a reward. If the animal lives in an environment where offering unwanted behaviour at inappropriate times may be met with punishment or aggression this will lead to conflict in the animal's mind which can cause a number of issues such as redirected aggression, avoidance or stress.

Equines that problem solve well may not always be willing to do what their trainer wants, instead choosing their own self directed behaviours. Thinking equines may solve problems that their trainer does not want them to solve, such as how to undo the stable catch and escape. Provided the trainer is prepared and the environment allows for a thinking equine then there should be no problems. Before beginning clicker training it is important to ask whether you are the sort of trainer who can accept and deal with the thinking, challenging, and problem-solving equine calmly and positively and without the interference of ego. If you can, then start clicker training.

Trainer limitation number 1

There a number of situations in which the skills and abilities of the trainer limit the effectiveness of clicker training and these should be carefully considered before starting training.

If a potential clicker trainer does not understand the science behind the use of clicker training then their abilities will reach a natural barrier to continued success. To get the best from a tool such as clicker training the user has to understand its application in order to understand how the equine may perceive what is happening.

There are a lot of trainers who do not understand the principles of reinforcement or schedules of reinforcement but they seem to do all right with their clicker training. There are also quite a few trainers who have had a go at clicker training only to give it up because they did not understand it or, due to incorrect use, they did not get the results they were expecting. However, if a trainer knows about the science of behaviour then the chances of success are much greater. By understanding what is happening those trainers who do all right with clicker training could do really well and those who gave up could have succeeded.

It does not take much to grasp the principles involved. Just read a good book, or attend a workshop on the science of behaviour and it will benefit not only the trainer's ability with the clicker but their skill in all areas of equine training. Incorrect use of the clicker can lead to confusion, frustration and even aggression in both equine and trainer so it is best to take the time to study the process before beginning.

Trainer limitation number 2

Clicker training should not be used as a quick fix for equine behavioural problems. There is a growing trend in the horse world for owners to attend demonstrations and at the end of the evening come away with a new tool to use on their animal. Essential to the success of clicker training is the animal's need to learn how the process works in order to understand how to receive rewards. So to buy a clicker and take it home and go straight to the trailer to fix the loading problem is unwise. If a trainer just wants to use it as a quick fix they are very likely to be sadly disappointed.

Trainer limitation number 3

Sometimes clicker training is seen as a positive way of get an equine to "like" the trainer. Equines that seem distant or shut down may well respond well to the use of clicker training. However, if we are using it just to build a bond there is the real danger that our timing and consistency will suffer as we search to reward every tiny behaviour so that the horse will like us. The moment that the animal shows some frustration with learning or at the click being withheld, the trainer's tendency is to give the reward anyway, thereby beginning the slippery slope into the horse demanding what they want and doing very little to get it.

We cannot make an equine like us and, even if we could, that is not really what we need in the human/equine relationship. What we want is a relationship of mutual trust and respect and this is gained through consistency, calmness, and persistency, all of which are learned or gained by doing things together. If we imagine a child constantly giving their "friends" sweets so they will be liked, we know where this will lead. A relationship dependent on giving treats means that once there are no sweets the true nature of the relationships can be seen. Inappropriate use of clicker training in this way will mask the true nature of the equine's trust and commitment to the human. I know using clicker training will enhance the relationship with the human far more than the use of punishment, but this cannot be the sole reason for using it.

Trainer limitation number 4

One of the main reasons a trainer should not use clicker training is if their timing is persistently poor. Timing is our communication when we work with equines and if our timing is poor then the animal is in big trouble. Timing can relate to the movements and control of our body language and the use of punishment, negative or positive reinforcement. In training, if our timing is consistently late, even by just one or two seconds, then we interfere with the messages we communicate to the animal. One of the greatest assets of clicker training is the possibility of perfect timing even from a distance, but this accuracy depends purely on the trainer's skill.

In order to have great timing the trainer must be able to connect with the animal in a way that allows the trainer to predict the animal's actions and thereby reward the behaviour as it happens. Timing requires concentration, awareness and practice. If a trainer has poor timing with other methods, is often slow to react or does not connect to the animal, then clicker training is something that should be avoided until the trainer's timing improves.

How do we improve timing? Practice is the only way to improve. Start with a video recording of a training session and observe and accept where improvements may be needed. Practise with a bouncy rubber ball thrown into the air and click each time it hits the floor. Practise the training game with family members, who can be more forgiving, before moving on to other species such as dogs and cats. Then start with simple behaviours with equines, such as targeting.

Sometimes the clicker can become overused by the trainer to maintain control over the animal. In fact they can over condition the animal creating an animal that appears controlled and calm when in fact they are simply offering the appropriate behaviours. This can lead to misreading the animal's temperament and intentions and that leads to over familiarity and accidents.

Clicker training is a tool to be used to aid learning. It should then be removed from training as each required behaviour is learnt. Often clicker trainers never finish the removal of the clicker from the training as they fear the animal will not perform the behaviour if the click is removed. The clicker is not an aid to control the animal, but is an aid to learning, and its continued overuse should be avoided.

As I have said before, my general rule for the use of clicker training to solve behavioural problems by novice or nervous horse owners is, "If you are not competent to work with an equine behavioural problem without a clicker, then don't work with the problem using a clicker."

In general we should not use clicker training wherever there is a danger we will mask other behaviours. This can lead to an animal that is controlled but misunderstood and therefore potentially dangerous.

I do not want to put people of using this excellent method of training. I just want trainers to be aware of the potential problems and pitfalls so they can be avoided, thereby ensuring the animals benefit most from clicker training. Used in the wrong situations it could appear that the method itself is faulty and this is not an image I want to portray to equine enthusiasts. Clicker training is only as good as the hands that hold it and the brains that work the hands.

It could be used by a good, experienced trainer in any of the prohibitive equine areas discussed in this chapter but a poor trainer with bad timing, and the wrong motivations, would not be able to use it safely even with a straightforward animal without the danger of creating problems. But I guess that goes for almost any equine training method.

CHAPTER 8

Can I use clicker training in conjunction with my other training methods?

A common phenomenon in the equine training world is the almost evangelical following that some trainers and methods attract. Clicker training and positive reinforcement have been no different. The early advocates of clicker training were naturally enthused by the incredible response their horses were having to clicker training. Clicker training has been claimed by some as the answer to all equine problems and that 100 per cent positive reinforcement was the only way to train. A clicker training advocate can be so enthusiastic that they only recommend the use of clicker training to the exclusion of any other training. But is this enthusiasm misplaced?

Horses have taught me that it is better to have ten solutions to one problem, rather than one solution to ten problems. Therefore, I have never advocated just one method or tool as being the only way of training equines. Equines are all individuals and so are their handlers. Consequently, as much as I believe clicker training is a great method of training and communication with equines, I do not recommend only clicker training. There are situations when I do not advocate the use of clicker training either because of the trainer's lack of skills or the animal's behaviour.

There are three ways in which trainers tend to use clicker training:

- 100 per cent clicker training and positive reinforcement in all aspects of their horsemanship
- clicker training just for problems and new behaviours
- clicker training for tricks and fun with the animal.

100 per cent clicker training

By claiming to use 100 per cent clicker training and positive reinforcement these trainers mean that they do not use any other form of recognised training method with their animals. They also claim to avoid any use of punishment or negative reinforcement with their animals.

Scientifically, it is virtually impossible to use 100 per cent positive reinforcement to train any animal. Even with clicker training there is a balance between positive and negative information. If the animal is rewarded for their behaviour this is positive reinforcement. However, if they are not rewarded for a behaviour, because it is considered to be incorrect by the trainer, then the silence created by the absence of the click provides negative information. The silence is saying, "Wrong, try again." In effect the trainer is trying to diminish the occurrence of the wrong behaviour and this would be considered scientifically to be punishment by removal or omission training, sometimes called negative punishment. Obviously the animal's perception of the situation and level of frustration at not receiving the expected reward would determine whether the withholding of a reward would constitute punishment.

To increase any occurrence of an established behaviour, withholding the reward is required to increase the animal's activity in search of the reward. This creates a frustration in the animal that it may want to avoid or escape from. However mild the frustration might be, it causes the animal to work to remove the frustration and receive the reward. This frustration could be considered a negative reinforcer.

Once the clicker is used to establish the required behaviour, the idea is to phase out its use for that behaviour. Then the maintenance of the behaviour relies on the schedule of reinforcement used and the method of communicating effectively which behaviour is required and when. At this point we see that in practice clicker training is always used along side other methods of communication. The most common form of complementary communication is our body language. Even 100 per cent clicker trainers are communicating with their animals using their body language much of the time.

Clicker training is so effective because it has a balance of negative and positive information. The clicks and the silence provide detailed information on what works and what does not work. Through the years of working with clicker training I have learnt that, technically, it is not 100 per cent positive.

Clicker training for new behaviour and problems

Some trainers just use clicker training for removing problem behaviours or creating new behaviours. The rest of the time they use their body language or negative reinforcement to communicate with the animal.

A trainer may use the clicker to teach the horse to load into the trailer but continue to use their other methods of training to work with the animal in other areas of training. The success of this approach depends on the other methods of training that are being used. Clicker training requires the animal being trained to learn to think and to solve problems. The positive nature of clicker training creates the motivation for the animal to offer behaviours without the fear of aversive consequences.

On the other hand, punishment-based training, or those methods using consistently high levels of negative reinforcement, cause the animal to be more hesitant to offer behaviours for fear of the consequences.

If a trainer uses clicker training for problems or new behaviours, yet uses punishment or heavily negative reinforcement based methods during training for ground work or riding, the animal may have to deal with a conflict between wanting to offer behaviour and being worried by the possible consequences of that behaviour.

Through consistent use of each method of training, and by using clear signals to inform the horse what type of training is being used and what behaviour is expected, the horse may cope with the conflict between the two methods of training. However, it is a real risk that the conflict between the different reactions required will cause stress due to the conflict the animal feels.

If the trainer uses body language and other methods of positive reinforcement, such as scratches, during the rest of the training then there should be no problem with mixing these different training methods. Both types of training encourage thinking and reward required behaviour. The animal does not have to fear the consequences of the behaviour, so these two types of training may actually complement each other.

Clicker training of tricks and fun

The types of trainer who use this approach generally already have a well established relationship with their animals and just want to add more fun to the relationship by increasing the animal's learning and problem solving skills. This type of clicker trainer does not usually have any problems, and their horses already do what that is asked of them. Again, provided the rest of the animal's training is mainly positive and encouraging, there is no problem in mixing clicker training with generally positive horse relationship.

In these three examples of the use of clicker training, the tendency is to have separate lessons for clicker training and other training methods. This allows the horse to better understand what is required of it in any particular lesson. My experience has been that, provided the other methods are positive or if negative reinforcement is used that it is not excessive, and does not escalate to heavy physical pressure, it is possible to use clicker training alongside different methods of training.

I do not recommend directly mixing clicker training with an aversive method of training in the same lesson. It may be tempting for trainers to try and increase the effectiveness of their training method by adding clicker training straight in to existing training methods. This usually happens with negative reinforcement based training methods, where, as the pressure is released, the trainer clicks in order to mark the correct behaviour. My belief is that this is neither effective nor necessary. Releasing the pressure and providing a click at the same time provides the animal with two pieces of information simultaneously. Rather than giving twice as much information as the trainer had intended, one of these messages will override the other. Which one is dominant will depend on the individual nature of the horse. The nervous horse will worry more about the aversive stimulus, and the highly food-motivated animal may take no notice of the aversive stimulus in favour of the click. We humans find it difficult to consider two pieces of information at the same moment and so do horses, donkeys and mules.

Imagine touching a hot kettle and as the pain causes you to pull your hand away rapidly someone clicks to reward the movement of your hand away from the kettle. As nice as the reward might be, the heat of the kettle has already taught the lesson most effectively, and you are unlikely to touch the hot kettle in future just to be able to pull you hand away in the hope of receiving a reward. The pain of the hot kettle overrides the positive reinforcement.

If the clicker is used in conjunction with a method that creates pain through aids such as the whip, spur, rope or bit, then the animal will be more concerned with the avoidance of pain than with receiving a small piece of carrot. In this situation the click could actually become reverse conditioned with pain and this would give the clicker a negative association, not a positive one.

I prefer to only use one signal at a time. If I have a donkey that does not like to have their hind legs handled, then my hands on their legs will be perceived by the donkey as nega-tive, and the removal of my hands as negative reinforcement. If I want to use clicker training to help this donkey they will first have to be rewarded for standing still. When I put my hands on the animal and the donkey remains still with all four feet on the ground I click and remove my hand, giving the reward of food. I do not try to click as I am removing my hand from the donkey's body. The click marks the behaviour of standing still as correct, but my hand should still leave the donkey's body while they are standing still, to ensure they learn standing still works, but the removal of my hand is sec-ondary and follows the click.

The only way this can be successful is if I use a shaping plan with small steps that allows the animal to be slightly uncomfortable, but not so uncomfortable that fear causes them to kick out. On balance, the click has to be more rewarding and motivating to the equine than the aversive stimulus is uncomfortable or frightening..

Clicker training creates equines that think, problem-solve, challenge and ask questions of the trainer. If the trainer uses other methods of training that rely on the animals doing what they are told, when they are told, this can cause conflict in the equine mind and lead to confusion, stress, and maybe even some unwanted stress-relieving behaviours.

Clicker training is very effective and very motivating for the animal, so there is no need to try and improve it by adding a negative or aversive stimulus because withholding the click is sufficient. Trainers who add clicker training directly to an aversive method are trying to improve the aversive method. Perhaps it would be better to avoid the aversive method in the first place if it needs the clicker to improve it.

If clicker training is used in conjunction with other positive methods of training and sympathetic body language then it does not have to be an all or nothing system of training. The use of clicker training depends on the individual equine and the situation. It is a tool that can be used for all training or more periodically if the other methods of training in use are complementary to the process of clicker training. The frequency of the use of this tool really depends on the individual trainer's beliefs and abilities. It can be mixed with other good training practices but it would be advisable to leave it in the tack box if aversive training methods are also in use.

CHAPTER 9

What is the difference between clicker training horses, donkeys and mules?

There is no difference in the application of the science of clicker training between horses, donkeys or mules, but there is a difference in their behaviour. This difference is best captured in an old saying about training equines: "You can tell a horse what to do, ask a donkey and negotiate with a mule." In my experience this saying is very true. However, I work on the principle that it is safer and more successful to negotiate with all three.

Horses have evolved with a finely tuned flight mechanism. The trainer's ability to harness and control this flight mechanism forms the basis of many horse training methods. The flight mechanism can be engaged to drive the horses away from the trainer. This way they discover they cannot escape from the trainer. This method of using the flight mechanism is the basis of many of the round pen training methods that are common today. A horse's fear and reaction to a painful or novel stimulus can be used to create movement which can then be used to force the horse to deal with the problems they face.

Donkeys evolved in a different environment to horses and have the potential for different types of social interaction. If there is plenty of vegetation and water they may form small harem herds. These donkey herds are more transient and more territorial than horse bands. In contrast, if donkeys live in an environment that has little water and sparse vegetation they lead more solitary lives. Mares will live on their own or with last year's offspring and during the breeding season stallions hold a territory near a watering hole which they defend from other males.

In domestication, the behavioural differences between horses and donkeys start to show. Donkeys can be territorial in their paddocks and it is not unheard of for them to attack small livestock and pets. Obviously, not all donkeys act in this territorial or aggressive way. Some are happy to live with live-stock such as chickens, goats or sheep. Due, possibly to their evolutionary environment and differing social structure, don-keys seem to have developed a stronger fight instinct than the horse. This fight instinct is strong enough for donkeys, in some parts of the world, to be used to defend herds of sheep and goats against canine predators.

The other differences between horses and donkeys are in their tolerance to pain, and their reaction to fear. Donkeys are very stoic animals that do not show pain readily. Their sto-icism is often so great, that even with a painful condition, the only visible symptoms may be a very small change in behav-iour. Horses tend to show their intolerance for pain much more readily, at early stages of illness. For this reason, it can be easy for trainers used to looking after horses to over look a painful condition in a donkey.

Donkeys are also less obvious with their display of fear or worry at new or frightening situation, making it easy for horse handlers and trainers to misread the donkey's body language. It is easy to see when a horse is fearful – their increasing ani-mation, widening eyes, flared nostrils, attempts to escape and general body language communicate their fear very clearly. Donkeys' on the other hand, are much more restrained in their response to fearful situations. Donkeys tend initially to plant their feet, raise their heads and widen their eyes only slightly. To the trainer unfamiliar with donkey body language it appears the donkey is only slightly interested in the situation when compared to the reaction of a horse.

The donkey's suppressed response to fear is what may have earned it the reputation for being stubborn and difficult to handle. When faced with a fearful situation, horses clearly demonstrate the high levels of anxiety they feel and the trainer can easily recognise their fear. A donkey may only show what appears to be mild interest or concern in fearful situations. This apparent absence of fear leads the inexperienced donkey handler to believe the animal is just "trying it on" or "just being stubborn". This is not the case. It is just a difference in the behaviour of the two species.

The old image of the donkey with a carrot dangling from a stick in front of them, tempting the stubborn donkey to move, actually has a degree of irony about it. While I would not advocate bribing the donkey, the use of positive reinforcement can be very motivating for a donkey or for any equine.

When donkeys do show their fear by barging past their handler it is often mistaken for a deliberate act of aggression by naughty or pushy donkey. This is probably because we are so unused to seeing a donkey react with fear that we forget they are flight animals as well. Many fearful or nervous donkeys are labelled as bad because trainers fail to recognise the donkey's escape reaction as fear.

Mules have a combination of their parents' traits. It is said, "If you can train a horse, you can train a horse, but if you can train a mule, you can train just about anything." Mules are more difficult to train because they can offer both donkey and horse behaviour. Having spent the first six months of their lives with their horse mother, they tend to be a strong mixture of her flight mechanism and their donkey father's stoic nature. This tends to mean we get an animal that appears strong and courageous but can be very fearful. This can lead the mule to appear calm and to be coping with the situation and a few seconds later the animal is trying to use its flight mechanism to escape when apparently nothing has changed.

Mules are not stubborn, but they do have a great sense of self preservation. A mule cannot be forced to do something it believes to be detrimental to its health. Anyone who says mules are stubborn has simply been outsmarted by one. They are quick to learn and willing to work with the trainer but they do have to be negotiated with.

Mules often demonstrate their mixed ancestry when being caught by a stranger for a unpleasant task. Initially, they may engage their mother's flight instinct and run away. However, once cornered or caught they offer the more stoic behaviour of their donkey father. Their self preservation tends to make them compliant giving rise to the impression that their previous flight reaction was them trying to deliberately deceive the trainer. If the treatment continues and the mule's comfort zones are exceeded then the mother's flight instinct is reengaged and panic appears to set in. These rapid changes in behaviour confuse most inexperience mule handlers and hence the mule is misunderstood.

In essence, all three species behave in different ways when being handled and this leads to the potential differences in their training. To succeed with each one we have to think with their unique species brain, not our own logical human brain.

If we are training donkeys, horses and mules without a clicker then the training methods used can be different with each species. "Natural Horsemanship" methods that rely on driving the horse away are not particularly successful with most donkeys and mules, as their flight mechanism is different from that of the horse. Aggressive methods of training tend to lead the donkey or mule to become fearful of the trainer or to fight back in response to the attempts to dominate them.

If the trainer uses the science of behaviour, positive reinforcement and successive approximation then it is possible to train all three using the same approach.

Clicker training is based on the science of behaviour and for that reason is extremely successful for horses, donkeys and mules. The principles can be applied in the same way for each species and the process of teaching the rules of clicker training is also the same.

The trainer does have to be aware of the differences of behaviour in each species and to compensate for the flighty nature of the horse compared to the donkey. As mules and donkeys tend to show their fear less obviously, the trainer needs to be aware of the smallest changes in the animal's body language in order to communicate effectively.

Clicker training does not rely on force to make the animal learn. To be successful, clicker training requires the development of the animal's problem solving skills and the positive, motivating nature of clicker training means that horses, donkeys and mules can all benefit greatly from its use.

CHAPTER 10

What do I need to get started?

"A bad workman always blames his tools, but isn't it funny how the best workmen have the best tools." At first it would seem that the only tool needed for clicker training is the clicker itself. It is possible to commence clicker training with just a clicker and a few carrots, but just like the good workman the good clicker trainer needs the best tools.

Bum bags and waistcoats

The bum bag or waistcoat is an essential piece of equipment for safe clicker training. We looked in detail at the use of bum bags or waists coat in the chapter on "Doesn't using food rewards cause equines to bite?' However, to briefly recap; two things happen when we use either a bum bag or waistcoat specifically for clicker training. Firstly, our pockets stop smelling of food so the animal stops constantly searching for food rewards in them, even when we are not clicker training and, secondly, the animal can become clearly aware of when food rewards are available and, more importantly, when they are not. This means that the animal learns to relax when rewards are clearly not available and that they do not continually offer all their learnt behaviours during every human interaction in the hope of being rewarded. The bum bag or waistcoat becomes a "clicker training and food rewards are available" signal.

The main factors influencing the choice of bum bag are

quite simple. The bag should be clearly visible to the animal being trained and some colour may help in this process, especially if it is a colour that will not normally clash with the trainer's clothing. If we are using a waistcoat, this should be distinctive but it is not necessary to use fluorescent colours which may be a little too visually stimulating to the animal.

When choosing a bum bag or waistcoat ensure there are several pockets with easy access for different types of rewards that might be used during a session. Bum bags often have the advantage of zips which keep out searching noses during the very early stages of clicker training. To prevent providing the animal with an unexpected jackpot, zips also stop rewards falling out on to the floor as the trainer bends over to pick up a foot.

The other important factor is that bum bags are regularly cleaned. Often bum bags are left in the tack room between sessions with any unused sliced vegetables slowly decomposing within. Hygiene is important and being able to wash or replace a bum bag before it becomes a health hazard is essential.

There are a number of especially designed treat bags or pouches on the market, primarily for dogs, and these can be used. However, do find one with several pockets. Their only other drawback of pouches is that they hang on the belt of the trainer and have a drawstring top. In my experience, this sometimes makes fast, easy access difficult. But it is a matter of personal choice.

Food Rewards

Having got something suitable to carry the rewards we then need to decide on the rewards to be used. Probably the first area of concern for any equine clicker trainer is the calorific effect of rewards on the animal's waistline. Obviously, low sugar, high fibre rewards are nutritionally safest. Unfortunately, the most fibrous forages are either difficult to use as a reward or not highly motivating for the animal. Timing the training session to coincide with when the animal will be motivated by even low value food is a good way to combat the problem.

If a pony is on restricted grazing then using some bagged forages designed for laminitics can be an effective reward. If the pony's fence is moved daily, pick some grass that they would normally eat and use it in the training session before moving the fence.

Equines on any form of supplementary feed can have part of their normal ration used in the clicker training session. This ensures they do not increase their food intake and spreads their food throughout the course of the day.

The variety and size of the reward is an important factor in increasing and maintaining the animal's motivation and influences the length and structure of training sessions.

If the trainer is unsure of their equine's order of preference for rewards, a little experiment can usually clarify the situation. Scattering a small quantity of different possible rewards, in a clean, dry concrete area or stable allows the animal to choose the rewards they find most valuable. If the animal eats everything with no observable preference, repeat the process a few days later and if the result is the same accept they just like them all. Ensure that all the rewards in the test are familiar to the animal. Avoid offering completely novel items in this test as the animal may require a while to develop a taste for new foods. Use the foods they showed a preference for intermittently during training to maintain motivation during learning and as jackpots to finish the session.

The value to the animal, of some rewards depends on the environment in which they are kept. Equines have a need for some items such as hay or grass at a consistent level. Other novelty rewards may initially promote a high-response rate from the animal but, when satisfied, the animal's motivation and behavioural responses drop.

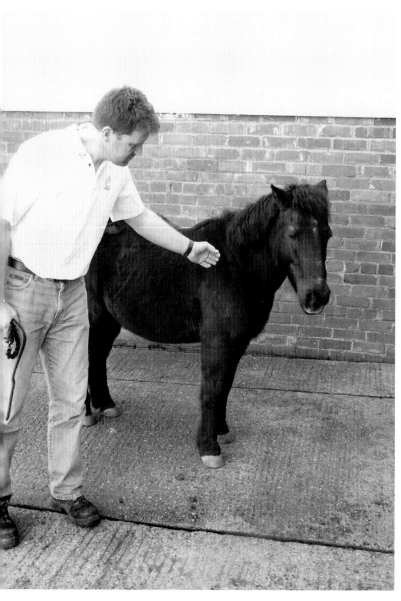

metimes fear of humans must be overcome before clicker training begins.

Marking the correct behaviour is easy using a marker signal.

Without the marker signal there is confusion over which behaviour is rewarded, feet up or feet down?

Differences between dogs and horses mean clicker training needs to be refined accordingly.

t is the timing of the food, not the food itself that causes equines to bite.

Sometimes safety precautions must be taken when starting clicker trainin

Typical size reward used for a horse, donkey or mule.

Different types of target.

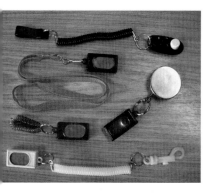

Some of the different ways of securing the clicker.

Some of the many different clickers available.

Starting clicker training targeting.

Starting clicker training with standing still.

Jackpotting the animal to finish a session.

Horse observing the trainer's hand movemen

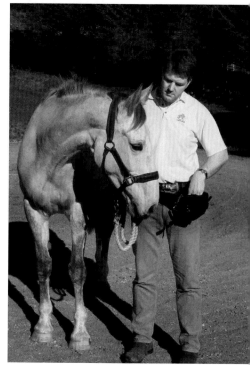

Horse responding as trainer's hand approaches the bum bag.

click

click

Extending the click and
delaying the reward.

delay

reward

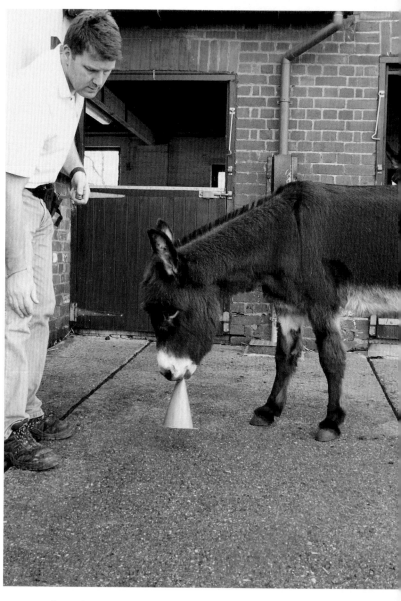

Learning an easy second task, such as picking up an object.

Mrs Knox, a clicker trained five-year-old mule.

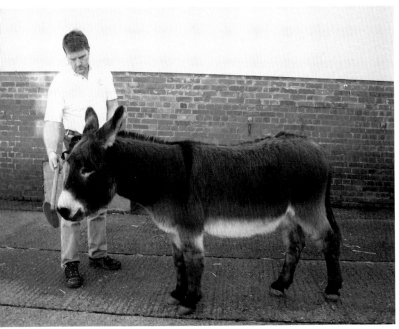

Jack, a clicker trained twenty-year-old donkey.

Using targeting to create head lowering.

Using pressure to create head lowering.

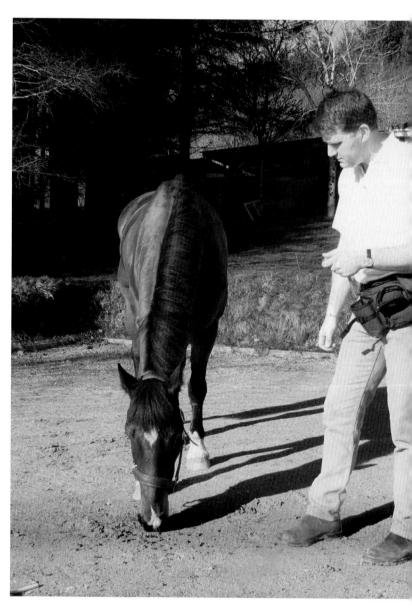

Using free shaping to create head lowering.

Using three different rewards during a session can help to maintain the animal's motivation. This might be a mixture of high fibre cubes and carrots, with pieces of apple for jackpots. This will of course depend on the animal's preferences for rewards, but using a mixture in this way can help keep the overall calorie intake down.

Foods that can be used include carrots, apples, parsnips, swedes, high-fibre nuts, short-chop-fibre bagged products, fresh grass, grass nuts, specially designed equine treats or whatever an individual animal has shown a liking for. Rewards such as ginger biscuits, which are particularly popular with donkeys, and mints and coarse or cool mixes should really only be given in small quantities to mark excellent work or as a jackpot to end the session.

Unlike dogs who can gulp their rewards down in seconds, equines need time to chew theirs. Hence the size of the reward is very important to the flow of the training session. If the reward is too big, the training session takes a long time while the trainer waits for the animal to finish chewing and then start looking for the next reward. It is also important to remember that even high-value rewards have a limit on how much the animal can consume. So, if the trainer is using half a carrot as a reward, the session will take longer and the animal's motivation is likely to decrease after carrot number four. Yet the total training session might only have consisted of eight reinforcements. Normally in a session we would expect to use a total of twenty to thirty rewards, including the jackpot.

The size of the animal has an effect the size of the reward. Obviously the cat will require a reward the size of a little fingernail and the elephant will require a whole bun for each reward. For a fifteen hand horse I use circle of carrot the size of a fifty pence piece, one centimetre thick, cut in half. This is equivalent to half a segment of apple or two or three high-fibre cubes. Perhaps a Shetland will require slightly less and a Shire slightly more

If the animal to be trained is overweight, not motivated by food, food aggressive or the trainer does not want to use food, then scratches in certain areas of the animal's body can be a very efficient substitute for food rewards. Scratching mimics the mutual grooming and is especially effective when the animal is more itchy during moulting in the spring. Each animal is unique so they will have different preferences for scratches. Generally, the withers, neck, mane or rump are the most favoured sites. A little trial and error may be required to find the animal's preferred scratching spot.

Scratching areas such as the withers and rump has been shown to lower the heart rate of horses, thus helping to keep the animal calm. Obviously, scratches from a human are not primary reinforcers and the horse, donkey or mule has to learn to accept and value them before scratching can be used effectively. A nervous, unhandled animal may not view scratching as a reward, only and once trust has been built and the animal has accepted human touch will it become effective.

If I am using scratches for training I either wear a pair of leather gloves or use a rubber massager. Most equines enjoy slow hard scratches done with the tips of the fingers. When this is done with bare hands, the tips of the fingers become so hot that scratching has to stop to allow them to cool down. Leather gloves protect the ends of the fingers and prevent the nails from actually damaging the animal's skin. A rubber massager is very effective and does not become tired like the fingers will. There are several varieties on the market and it is a process of trial and error to find the one the animal likes most.

Scratches as a reward are most effective when used in five to six second bouts following the click. Ideally, I have found that if the trainer can get the animal to just start to show value in the scratch, by moving the head or arching the neck before stopping, then they remain motivated to work to for the next scratch.

Targets and toys

Teaching the animal to target is valuable in helping them to learn the process of clicker training and how to gain rewards.

A target can be something as simple as the coloured lid of a feed supplement tub. Small plastic cones sold for games and sports use also make very good targets. These cones are light enough to handle easily and they are usually quite colourful which helps to attract the animal's attention in the first few lessons. Cones can also be picked up by the animal, which is a behaviour that might be useful during the next stage of learning about clicker training.

Purpose made targets with handles can be bought or made. The use of a target with a handle does allow the trainer to stretch the animal's learning after the first few sessions by asking the animal to go further away from the food source to touch the target without overreaching the animal. Although one could speculate as to which colour an equine would find easiest to see, the colour of the target does not seem overly important.

Some trainers use their fist as a target for the animal to touch. I personally do not like to do this as I believe there is too much opportunity to confuse the animal. Most people are right handed and therefore hold their clicker in that hand, while the left hand is used to make the target and deliver the food. If the target hand smells of food, there is a real possibility that it will be harder for the animal to learn not to mug or invade the trainer's space in search of food. The animal may also be touching the hand in search of food, rather than learning to deliberately target an object to receive a reward.

Trainers who use their fist would argue that it is convenient as it is always available and much easier to use than an extra piece of equipment such as the cone. If the trainer's hand is a target, it is always in view and in close proximity to the horse, who may be tempted to target the hand when it is not required or to target other people's hands. As behaviour gets bigger before it changes, I feel there is a real danger that during the learning process horses could nip or bite the "target" as is common for them to do, and this could be very painful for the trainer. In addition to this, it can be confusing for the animal that sometimes has to target the hand and, at other times, is expected to ignore the hand and remain still while they are handled. Using a manufactured target is consistent and clear to the animal, and during any form of training we should always do what is best for the animal, not what is easiest for the trainer.

During the process of learning clicker training it can be helpful if there are some toys that can be used too. The need for these toys will depend on what the trainer wishes to teach the animal. Often, teaching the animal to pick something up or retrieve a thrown object can assist in the learning process. For this the target cone or an old soft hat are usually best. Obviously, any safe, suitably sized item can be used, but be aware that equines tend to find hard, dry items more difficult to pick up.

Controlling the clicker

One of the objections raised to using the clicker is the difficulty people find in using it while holding the lead rope, rewards and target. In the later stages of clicker training people find it difficult to use the clicker while picking up a hoof or using another piece of equipment at the same time. This problem is easily overcome by attaching the clicker to the bum bag and practising with it.

Attaching the clicker to the bum bag means it does not have to be held all the time. It can be dropped and it will hang there ready for use the moment it is required. Like any piece of equipment the use and control of the clicker requires some practice. Once familiar with its use the clicker is not a hindrance at all and is easy to use even while picking out feet. On a safety note, if you have the clicker attached to the bum bag, it cannot be dropped on the floor and either startle the animal or force the trainer to pick up the clicker by bending down in front of the animal, which could be dangerous.

There are a number of ways to attach the clicker to the trainer or the bum bag. It really is personal choice as to which feels most comfortable and easy to use. Different types of training situations might also benefit from different types of connection.

Wrist coils are a simple elastic rubber coiled loop that fits over the wrist like a bracelet and clips on to the clicker. These are good for riding or if the trainer does not want to reach for their clicker. The length of the coil and the size of the trainer's wrist can sometimes make the clicker a little difficult to pick up as it hangs from the coil.

Straight elastic rubber coils attach to the bum bag. The coil is about thirty centimetres long but stretches up to a metre, giving plenty of freedom of movement for the clicker. If let go these elastic coils do tend to spring the clicker back towards the bum bag at great speed, which can startle a nervous horse. I find that these attachments are essential for working with feet as they stretch enough, allowing me to hold the clicker while both hands are on the feet. When the clicker is dangling from the bum bag, it is in just the right place for easy access while one is still bent over.

A simple key chain or string on a retractable coil which attaches to the bum bag is another option. I have used the retractable chain, and the only disadvantages are that there is always tension on the clicker as the chain tries to recoil and that as they recoil they can be noisy.

Finger coils are a smaller version of the wrist coil, just looping an elastic material around one finger on the clicker hand. These loops can be good for riding or for feet work. It is not so easy to put these down to free up the clicker hand completely but never the less they can be very useful.

Some trainers use a neck lanyard to hang the clicker from. This is my least favourite option. While bending over to deal with feet the clicker tends to swing right out away from the body and dangle in the way. I also worry that having this loop around the trainer's neck could prove dangerous if the horse got a foot through it or a piece of equipment got caught up in it.

If the clicker is used for riding then either a finger coil or wrist coil is most suitable. If preferred the clicker can be taped to a fifteen centimetre piece of wooden dowelling rod or to the handle of a whip (the whip is not to be used as a whip but only for holding the clicker) so the rider can carry the clicker in a convenient place for its easy operation.

Clickers

Just like the methods of attaching the clicker to the bum bag there are a number of different types of clicker available, but the basic principle is the same. They are nearly all just a plastic box with a metal strip inside. The click sound is produced as the metal is flexed and straightened. Some clickers require direct pressure to the metal strip, others have a button to press that operates the metal strip. Clickers now come in a wide range of colours as well as transparent, two tone, and fluorescent. They are found in different shapes but as far as I can tell, equines do not mind what colour or shape the clicker is.

Some clickers are plain, being designed only to be held in the hand. So it is important when buying a clicker to ensure it has a tab for connecting to the chosen method of control. Other than that it really is a matter of personal choice as which feels most comfortable and which sound suits the trainer and equine best. Each type of clicker has a slightly different tone. Some produce a very sharp loud click which is almost painful to hear, others produce a softer, more pleasing sound. Unfortunately, I am unaware of any research that would help us to determine which sounds equines prefer.

On my training courses, when we use a clicker in the training game, I give the participants a choice of clickers and ask them to choose the one they feel sounds most pleasing and it is almost always a softer click in the middle of the volume range. Often the horses, donkeys and mules I have clicker trained have learned to put their ears back during training. They certainly do not seem displeased at the process of clicker training, so I have often wondered if the sound and volume of the click is too loud at such close proximity, causing them to put the ears back to soften the sound or lower the volume.

Apart from the normal plastic and metal box clickers, there are now a variety of others clicker available. There are volume control clickers which have a choice of three noise levels acti-vated by moving a small plastic slide on the back.

I personally like to carry in my bum bag a small toy bug clicker which makes a sharp but low volume sound which can be used for equines nervous of the click.

There are several button clickers on the market. The button clicker has several advantages over the plain clicker: it can be operated with any part of the hand, making it ideal for riding or for winter use when gloves are worn. It can be held in the fist and operated to deaden the sound for the nervous animal. The sound is not too harsh and it is easily attached to any type of coil.

There are even electronic clickers that have a variety of sounds made electronically with two volume settings. This really is the height of technology for the clicker. The idea is that different animals can be trained with each of the four dif-ferent sounds or that animals could be trained using two sounds to mark behaviour and jackpot behaviour differently. I personally have found this a little too complicated for use with equines but perhaps with a pack of dogs it could be very helpful.

I would also recommend that the bum bag always has a spare clicker in it so that lost, broken or dropped clickers do not stop the training session in the wrong place.

The choice of which tools to use is really down to the indi-vidual but I would say that to clicker train effectively a bum bag with a clicker attached to it is essential. I would advise any trainer to find what they and their animal find most comfortable to use. Fortunately, unlike most equine training products, clicker and the associated equipment is very cheap so the trainer can afford to try different tools and clickers with minimal expense.

CHAPTER 11

Do I have to use a clicker?

Over the years, many people have asked me if they have to use a clicker at all. Trainers have told me that they use a word or a tongue click in place of the clicker. They claim to use voice clicks or words because they find it difficult to use the clicker and coordinate their hands, bum bag, target and horse while concentrating on what the animal is doing. They also say the voice is always available and therefore more useful. I would argue that following my instructions regarding bum bags and clicker attachments the use of the clicker becomes easier, even for beginners. Easy use of the clicker is attainable for everybody, it is simply a matter of accepting that initially using the tools of clicker training will feel uncomfortable but with persistent practice the clicker can become a comfortable extension of the trainer's hands.

Scientifically, a trainer can use any consistent signal to act as a bridge between a behaviour and a reward. With training and good timing any signal could be effective. However, I have been using clickers for almost ten years with horses, donkeys and mules and if using a tongue click or word was more successful then I hope I would be smart enough to start using it instead of the clicker. Trainers who use voice clicks often want to be reassured that they are doing the right thing and, at the same time they do not want to hear that using a clicker is more effective than the tongue click or word.

There are a number of reasons that I believe the best tool for the job is the neutral stimulus provided by the clicker. The first reason I prefer to use the clicker is that it allows the trainer to see their timing more easily than a tongue click does. Seeing timing is a difficult concept to understand, but essentially it means observing the gap between the animal's behaviour and the trainer's response to that behaviour. Even novices with no experience in clicker training can see whether a click arrived during the intended behaviour or whether it was late. This is something that is more difficult to do using the voice or tongue click. The sharpness of the sound coming from the clicker seems easy to observe as it is independent of the trainer's body. Clicker trainers are notorious for wincing as they miss the desired behaviour by hundredths of a second. Yes, we can see the timing of the tongue click compared to the behaviour but we do not always observe it. As the tongue click comes from within us and is personal to us it carries our emotional desire to mark a behaviour and, therefore, the edges of our perception become blurred. If our timing is late with the clicker we are just late with a bridging signal. It is not personal. If we are late with the tongue click we ourselves could feel we are wrong. We do not like being wrong so we tend not to observe the timing of the tongue click as persistently as we do with the mechanical clicker. It is really only if a trainer has spent time using a clicker that they can experience the benefits a clicker brings in this way.

Timing is the key to communication, so without out good timing the communication is inaccurate and training will become less effective. So another benefit of using the clicker and the improved observation of timing is that the trainer's timing tends to improve considerably with the use of clicker. In American dog training schools where tongue clicks were compared to the use of the clicker in dog training classes, there is some evidence that when the clicker was used, the dogs and their owners increased their speed of learning by up to 50 per cent.

Another advantage of the clicker over a tongue click or word is that, no matter how hard we try, the emotional content of our mind affects the tone, strength and pitch of our voices. This emotional content of using the words yes, good or a tongue click means that we are providing a personal emotional connection rather than a neutral, mechanical unemotional sound. Even the tongue click has emotional content because it comes from us and therefore is affected by how we feel. The emotions attached to sounds or the emotional content of our voice influences our body language which further interferes with the message received by the animal. While the voice might say yes, the trainer's posture can be saying no. The clicker seems to have no emotional content and this frees it from the trainer's state of mind more than a tongue click. By marking the behaviour with a click the trainer decouples the emotional connection between right and wrong and replaces it with a signal that uniformly means success, rewards are coming. With less confusion we can speed up learning and reduce the stress of the animal and trainer.

People ask if it is alright to use the tongue click. Yes, it is all right to use the tongue click, providing they accept that they are placing limitations on a very good system of training. It is a bit like asking if it is all right to use a cricket bat to play golf. Technically, we can use a cricket bat to play golf and if we enjoy using a cricket bat to play golf that is fine, but we will never be a great golfer using a cricket bat, because a golf club is a far better tool to use for playing golf.

CHAPTER 12

How do I start clicker training?

The starting point for any potential clicker trainer is preparation for training. There are six steps to successful clicker training.

- Understand the science of clicker training and how it works. This knowledge leads to confidence in the training process which will create a more consistent trainer.
- Practise the training game on willing humans. This improves understanding of the process, teaches shaping more effectively and improves timing.
- Develop a shaping plan for the required behaviour. If the trainer does not know what they are doing, then how is the animal expected to know. Be clear and consistent about what is being taught.
- Create a safe environment for training and, do not take any risks or be tempted to take short cuts. Set the animal up to succeed.
- Take the steps from the shaping plan and prepare for the lesson. Having spent the time preparing fully, go out and start clicker training. Start learning and have fun.
- Teach the equine about clicker training.

How do I teach clicker training to my horse donkey or mule?

Having come straight from the dog training world, clicker training for equines has followed the same pattern of rewarding every click. This made scientific sense, because the animal needs to know the click is a reliable predictor of food arriving. Some trainers even went as far as to say if the trainer clicked and did not reward the animal, then the trainer was lying to the animal. When I first started clicker training equines, and when watching others clicker train their horses, one of the problems that I observed was how difficult it was to remove the clicker from training without causing frustration in the animal. As well as becoming frustrated, the animal could even become aggressive as the trainer started to withhold or remove the click or the reward. In general it was a slow process to gradually get the animal to perform the desired behaviour for slightly longer before the click arrived. Impatient or demanding horses were even more problematic.

During clicker training, the horse that is aware that rewards are available but is unaware how to acquire them may well show frustration activities. Knowing rewards are available but not knowing how to get them can cause a conflict in the emotional state of the animal. The horse lacking in patience will experience frustration which may lead to aggression or excitable behaviour. This frustration does demonstrate that the animal values clicker training and the rewards they receive highly.

This behaviour is similar to a horse in a stable on a reduced feed ration next to a horse eating a normal ration. When the horse on the reduced ration finishes their food they may become frustrated by their failed attempts to get to the food of their neighbour. This may lead to anxiety driven behaviours such as biting or pacing. If this situation continues for long periods, aggression may result from the stress that is created.

The other problem with my early clicker training experiences was the animal hearing the click and immediately looking for the food. The second they heard the click they would snatch their foot away from the trainer or instantly stop walking. There is even the classic story of the rider who clicked her horse for going over a low jump only to find that her horse stopped the instant it touched the ground on the other side in the hope of receiving the reward and due the speed of the stop, the rider fell off over the horse's shoulder.

The lack of patience and abrupt end of the behaviour made equine clicker training a potentially lengthy process and created some difficulty in extending the behaviours to a point where the clicker might be removed. In fact, some trainers never removed the clicker at all, preferring to continue using it for months, and in some cases years, for the same behaviours.

It seemed to me that equines are smarter than this and could be trained to be patient. By teaching the donkeys, horses or mules right from the start that patience is a natural part of the "game", they begin to become patient. This pays dividends later as the trainer begins to try and establish variable schedules of reinforcement and remove the clicker from the training procedures.

It was also obvious that donkeys, mules and horses were not dogs and that there should be some key differences in the ways of training them. By watching an excellent trainer with great timing clicker train equines, it became clear that altering how the animal learnt clicker training right from the start would make the process safer, faster and cause less frustration.

I also observed that equines continued to read our body language during clicker training sessions and that they were naturally receiving and understanding certain unconscious signals that all clicker trainers were using. As always the horses, donkeys and mules were the best teachers, all I had to do was to see the lesson.

It is vitally important, during the first session, to start introducing the animal to the concept of patience and the effects of variable schedules of reinforcement. Patience can initially be taught during the learning of a simple behaviour such as targeting or standing still. Equines are all unique individuals and the speed at which they progress will be dependent on their nature and previous experiences. Equines that have received positive training and are active and bold seem to learn faster than equines that have been in negative or aversive environment. This means that there is no ABC of teaching clicker training. The trainer must assess and work with each animal on a time scale that fits the individual animal.

Previously, the click had always been a terminal bridge and, it always ended the behaviour and meant food was coming. This predictability of the arrival of food is what leads to the snatching behaviour after click, and the frustration as the click is withheld. My process of clicker training is based upon the use of the clicker not as a terminal bridge but as an intermediate bridge or "keep going" signal.

To facilitate the clicker as an intermediate bridge, the animal must also be given another signal which they can use as a terminal bridge. I noticed that the animals I was working with had already established a terminal bridge for themselves. The terminal bridge the animals were waiting for was the movement of the trainer's hand towards the bum bag to retrieve a reward following the click.

This movement happened every time the animal was rewarded and was consistent throughout the lesson. In fact, if you watch any clicker-trained equine, they hear the click and then watch for the movement of the trainer's hand to the food store. They might hear the click and look around. If the hand does not move they shift their head back and wait. By deliberately using this movement of the hand to the bum bag as a terminal bridge we are able to use the clicker as an intermediate bridge. Straight away the conscious use of two signals enables us to teach patience to the horses, donkeys and mules.

The object of the exercise is to teach the animal at the very early stages of clicker training that a food reward may arrive immediately after the click or after several clicks. However, the food will always arrive after the trainer's hand goes to the bum bag.

Initially, the scientific objection to this procedure would be that, without an immediate reward, the click would lose its strength as a bridging signal. To prevent this from happening, the gap between the click and the movement of the hand to the bum bag must also be on a variable duration of reinforcement. This means that sometimes the click will be five to ten seconds before the movement of the hand to the bum bag and other times it will be only one second before. Because the click is sometimes closely associated with the reward it maintains its strength as a bridging signal. What makes this possible is that equines are very capable of learning the association between closely linked events and chains of events that lead to reinforcement.

For the equine to learn about clicker training and about patience, we start with a simple behaviour on a continuous sequence of reinforcement. A continuous schedule of reinforcement is where the consequence for a behaviour occurs every time the desired behaviour occurs. The first two behaviours I teach are either targeting or standing still.

Targeting requires the animal to touch an object for a reward and targeting can help an equine that has never really had their problem-solving skills developed. Touching a target to receive a food reward may not seem like a challenging behaviour for the equine brain. However, it never ceases to amaze me how difficult this simple procedure can be. To touch an object fifty centimetres from the food source makes no sense to an animal that is used to putting their head down to eat what they see.

Targeting teaches the animal to think and solve problems that they have never come across before. Targeting also teaches the animal that they have to do something in order to receive rewards. Stretching the target further and further from the food source gradually shapes the animal's problem solving skills. By the end of seven days of targeting most equines are capable of touching a target thrown three metres away from the trainer. Some may have even progressed to picking up the target, although this may take a while longer for some equines. The rate of learning depends on the individual's past treatment, personality and the trainer's ability.

Preferably, the target should be something the animal has not seen before so that their natural curiosity will cause them to explore the object. Obviously, the target should not be too scary or the animal may not want to touch it at all. If an equine is so nervous that it does not want to touch a novel object in this way, the trainer should reconsider if the animal is really ready to be clicker trained or if other training to give the animal confidence should take place first.

If the trainer is in any doubt about the reaction of the animal to the clicker or to food rewards then these early stages of training should be done in a safe environment that allows the trainer to step back out of the animal's space. This can be accomplished by training over a stable door, stable door chain, over a wall or post and rail fence.

Ideally, the first sessions should take place in an area where the animal feels comfortable and that is safe and free from distractions. With the horse, donkey or mule on a lead rope, start with the suitable target behind the trainer's back and carefully bring it forward in front of the animal. As they reach out to explore the target, click and reward.

Equines that already have good problem solving skills and readily offer behaviours for reinforcement can start clicker training by learning to stand still rather than with targeting, providing that being touched over their body is not an issue for them. Clicker training should never begin by working on problem behaviours. It is most successful when the animal is allowed to learn how clicker training works before they have to deal with their own fears and phobias as well.

Standing still should always be taught at the start of clicker training as it is a fundamental behaviour essential to so many domesticated behaviours. In most cases of behaviour problems, equines in general find it extremely difficult to calmly stand still and deal with problems that may be presented by the handler. Therefore, slow, confident handling, teaching the animal to stand quietly and calmly provides an excellent base for future learning whenever the animal encounters a problem. It is my belief that animals that are already reasonably happy to stand still also benefit from learning that standing still and being calm can be offered as an effective solution to difficult situations. However, it may not be advisable to initially train standing still to an animal that is unwilling to lead. In this case, targeting could be substituted for standing still.

Depending on the animal, clicker training can either start with targeting or standing still. However, if the training starts with targeting, standing still should always be taught once the animal has mastered standing still.

Normally, twenty to thirty rewards, including the jackpot, are sufficient for a training session. Many new clicker trainers make the mistake of enjoying the session so much, that they carry on and on until the animal loses interest or they run out of rewards. Shorter but good quality lessons are far more effective than long ones. It is better for the animals learning to have three sessions of five to eight minutes than one twenty minute session. If the animal performs brilliantly in the first thirty seconds of training, jackpot the behaviour and stop the training session there. Take a breather and, if required, come back to training a few minutes later.

Jackpots are used to mark excellent behaviour and the end of a session. The jackpot should be five to ten pieces of food, depending on the reward, in a rubber bucket or straight on to the ground. By using a jackpot in this way it gives the animal a clear "session finished" signal. This jackpot also gives the trainer a chance to move away and remove the bum bag or waistcoat before returning to the animal.

Just stopping the session and walking away because the trainer has finished or run out of rewards can be seen as punishment by the animal. As well as signalling the end of the training session, marking a desired behaviour with a jackpot reinforces that behaviour and increases the chances that the animal will understand what is required of them. (More details on the use of food reward and scratches as an alternative can be found in the chapter, 'What do I need to get started?')

A final word about rewards. Leave them in the bum bag until the animal has received the click. The trainer should not have the reward already in the hand during training as the smell and presence of the food may distract the animal and the movement of the hand to the bum bag will be at the wrong time.

Following the jackpot at the end of the first few sessions, it is important to take off the bum bag or training waistcoat and come back and interact with the animal so that they can learn the rule, that food rewards are available only when the bum bag or waistcoat is present. This process is explained fully under the chapter dealing with whether food rewards cause equines to bite.

To teach standing still, the trainer should begin by placing their hand on a part of the animal's body that they are sure the animal will be comfortable with. The hand should be held there until the animal is standing still with their head straight out in front of them. Then click and reward the behaviour.

This process of click and reward for either targeting or standing still should continue until the animal can be seen to look for the food reward when hearing the click. This shows the animal is making the association between click and food rewards or, more scientifically, between the primary reinforcer and the conditioned reinforcer. As this conditioning begins to occur, the trainer can check the process is developing by clicking and not moving their hand, waiting three seconds and then moving their hand to the bum bag. The animal should

103

continue to hold their head forward and only move once they see the movement of the hand towards the bum bag. This will demonstrate that the animal is associating not only the clicker to food, but the movement of the hand towards the impending food reward. In the early stages of learning, the animal may hear the click and move their head to receive the reward but if the trainer's hand does not move they will return their head to straight out in front.

If this association becomes established during the first session, providing the animal is exhibiting the correct behaviour, two clicks in quick succession, with a food reward following the second one, can be used. Then return to continuous reinforcement, finishing with a jackpot. This is usually sufficient for the first session. The progress to using two clicks is usually slower when teaching targeting compared with teaching standing still, as standing still is something the animal can already do whereas targeting has to be learned and understood first. The reason for using two clicks is to introduce the animal to the idea that clicker training is subject to variable schedules of reinforcement and that food does not follow after every single click but food always follows the movement of the trainer's hand to the bum bag.

It must be remembered that all equines will learn at different speeds and, for this reason, perseverance is sometimes required while the animal learns the concepts involved in gaining food rewards. Each equine has its own learning style and, despite the presence of food, some will still take several sessions before they become more animated and show they understand the process. It is important for the trainer not to panic and think that clicker training is not working. The trainer just needs to check they are doing everything right and then quietly continue to repeat session one. If after eight to ten good quality sessions the animal shows no sign of improvement then the trainer needs to consider changing, reward type, task or environment.

Sometimes, if the trainer is new to clicker training, the fault lies not with the animal but with the trainer, and therefore a video camera to record a couple of sessions for review afterwards can sometime throw light on the problem.

Once the animal has completed the first session level satisfactorily, during the second session repeat the steps from the first lesson for the first ten rewards then add in the double click. Following this, use the single click and then the double again. Begin to select a random order of rewards, after the first click, the third or the second. At this stage there can be up to three seconds between the clicks. The trainer's hand should go straight to the bum bag following the last click of each sequence. If the animal is working with targeting be sure that the animal is targeting consistently accurately before adding these double clicks, as the animal will have to touch the target for each click.

The third element of training is for the trainer to click following the required behaviour and wait for three to four seconds before moving the hand to the bum bag. This element can be introduced as early as the end of the second lesson with some animals, for others it may be the end of the third or fourth clicker session. The animal's calmness and speed of progress is the determining factor as to when to move on to this step. If teaching standing still, the trainer's hand should remain in contact with the area of the body until three or four seconds after the click, and the movement of the hand to the reward bag should occur while the required behaviour is still occurring. This begins to teach patience by teaching the animal not to expect a reward the moment they hear the click. It also confirms to the animal that the movement of the hand to the reward bag is a terminal bridge and the reward will always follow.

The targeting animal should be able to consistently touch the target two or three times and receive a click for each one before being rewarded. Then the delay in moving the hand to the bum bag for three to four seconds following the last touch and click can be introduced.

During the sessions of clicker training from this point on, the reward will always be delayed by anything up to eight seconds from the last click. This delay of the reward should always be on a variable schedule of reinforcement. Sometimes a one-second delay and some times an eight second delay or any time in between. This variation helps to maintain patience and allow the behaviour to be extended for longer because the animal does not know when to expect the reward. If the animal knows they have to wait for the hand to move to the bag before the reward will arrive they learn to wait. As they wait, another click can be given thereby resetting the duration of the behaviour before the terminal bridge ends the behaviour.

This system of introducing the clicker to horses, donkeys and mules is highly effective at producing animals that are patient while being clicker trained and are prepared for the removal of the clicker. We really need this patience in equines because they are generally big enough and powerful enough to injure the trainer if they get frustrated or start demanding food.

Many of the behaviours we teach an equine are duration behaviours. These are behaviours we want them to perform for longer. With the original click and reward every time method of clicker training the behaviour stops when the animal hears the first click which is OK if you are teaching behaviour which has a natural end, like stand still until I get on, or fetch the target. However, click and instant treat is not helpful for behaviours that need to be extended for longer periods, such as holding their food up for long or leading correctly for greater distances. With my new method of teaching clicker training, the click acts as a "keep going' signal and the hand movement acts as the terminal bridge and it is much easier for the animal to learn these duration behaviours.

As I have said before, all equines are individuals and this has to be taken into account. Some appear to be naturally patient. However, this should not be taken for granted and the same process should be followed to prevent problems later on in the training. Learning to be patient is also the process of the animal learning how clicker training works and this training is essential as the required behaviours become more complicated or challenging.

Once the delay-reward concept has been introduced, the same procedure should be followed for the subsequent three to five training sessions. Continuous reinforcement used for one or two clicks, depending on the ability of the animal, this is followed by a variable schedule with one or two clicks with delayed delivery of the reward before the trainer moves to a delayed schedule of reinforcement, where the reward arrives between one and eight seconds after the click. If a behaviour is suitable finish by offering clickless reward.

The clickless reward is the fourth stage of clicker training and is the final stage of removing the click altogether. Initially, an intermediate step can be used with the animal receiving two or three clicks for correct behaviour and the terminal bridge, the movement of the hand, being delayed for ten to twelve seconds after the last click but still occurring in conjunction with the desired behaviour. If the animal continues to work patiently for the rewards and the desired behaviour is maintained the final step can be introduced, the completely clickless reward. While the animal is performing the required behaviour the trainer's hand goes straight to the bum bag and the animal is rewarded.

The clickless reward can be used to reward established parts of the behaviour. If the behaviour is standing still and the animal has only just progressed to being touched on the hindquarters, but is now happy to stand while the neck is touched, a clickless reward can be used for the neck area while work on progressing past the ribs can use the click and delay of reward. This way the clicker is already being gently phased out while the animal learns about clickless rewards.

Once the behaviour is fully established the clicker is rapidly phased out and only clickless rewards need to be used and these too are reduced, then faded out to a long variable schedule of reinforcement.

While it might at first appear that this is a great deal for the trainer and animal to take in, one must remember the terminal bridge of the movement of the hand has always been observed by the animal being clicker trained. The movement of the trainer's hand to the bum bag can be used at all times, therefore, even with the clickless reward, the animal is still controlled by the operant conditioning exerted upon them by the movement of the hand. To be successful the trainer must be extremely careful about the timing of the movement of their hand to the bum bag throughout training.

If problems occur it is often because an individual animal has been overreached by lessons that have been too fast or timing that has been poor. If at any time the required behaviour of the animal begins to consistently diminish or the animal struggles with the next step of learning then go back a couple of steps on the process and spend one or two sessions ensuring that the animal is happy with that level of learning before moving on to the next step.

Providing that the trainer is consistent with their behaviour, and good with their timing, it is easy for the equine to pick up this system of clicker training. It is much easier to start to remove the click at the beginning of training than to work for two months with the animal receiving a reward after every click, so that the conditioning is really ingrained and then suddenly give the click a different meaning by withholding the click or not rewarding every click.

In conclusion, by using these techniques to train the donkey, horse or mule to be calm and to deal with the effects of a variable schedule or delayed schedule of reinforcement, one can accelerate the learning and prevent frustration and excitement-based behaviours that may occur in some equines during the traditional clicker training process. It allows the use of the clicker as an intermediate bridge, with the hand movement to the bum bag as a terminal bridge that finishes the behaviour. In effect, the clicker can be used as a "keep going" signal. This makes duration behaviours much easier to establish and the removal of the clicker from the training process quicker and at an earlier stage than previously possible.

It is important to realise that using the clicker in this way has to be learnt by the animal and, therefore, an extremely easy task should be selected for the training process. It is important that the animal clearly understands the rules and concepts surrounding the schedules of reinforcement and the availability of rewards before embarking on a training programme of more complicated behaviours. This can be likened to explaining the rules of a game carefully to a small child before starting to play; this does not mean to say that the small child will not attempt to break the rules but, with practice, he will understand that activities outside the rules are not reinforced. In a similar way, an equine exposed to these rules at an early stage will be more likely to exhibit patience without frustration later on.

A summary of the process of teaching clicker training

- Prepare for training.
- Continuous schedule of reinforcement, hand immediately to bum bag.
- Two clicks, hand immediately to bum bag.
- Check progress, click and don't move hand, watch animal response.
- Second session, first ten continuous reinforcement then increase to two clicks before reinforcement.
- Variable schedule of clicks, hand to bum bag after one, two or three clicks.
- Click and wait two to three seconds before hand moves to bum bag.
- Variable schedule of delay from click to hand to bum bag up to eight seconds.

- Introduce clickless reward.
- Consolidate learning of delayed reward and introducing clickless treat.

Continuing the process of learning

Having taught the animal how clicker training works, the next step is to train a simple non-confrontational behaviour that reinforces the animal's knowledge of how to receive rewards. If the animal has been target trained they can then be trained to stand still when handled or left by the trainer. If they have already been trained to stand still then target training can be useful as it has many possible application in later training.

The other common behaviour to train is picking up an object or fetching the object when thrown by the trainer. This is just a matter of shaping the animal's behaviour to target the object and, when that is established, withholding the reward until the animal begins to nibble or lick the target and then reward this behaviour. This way the animal can be quickly shaped to bite and then bite and lift the object. Once the animal has learnt this second behaviour the foundations are in place to work with any behaviour that is desired.

Once the horse, donkey or mule has learnt about the variable schedule of clicks, the delay from click to reward and the clickless reward during the training of the first behaviour , they do not need to be taught them again so the second behaviour is easier to teach. The trainer can start with single clicks with a short delay to the terminal bridge. As soon as the animal begins to offer the required behaviour, a variable schedule of clicks can be used to extend the behaviour with the delay of the terminal bridge. Following this , the clickless rewards can consolidate the learning and begin the removal of the clicker. This pattern can be repeated whenever a new behaviour is clicker trained.

Summary for the continuation of clicker training

- Create shaping plan for new behaviour.
- Single click continuous reinforcement with delayed terminal bridge.
- Soon as possible use variable schedule of clicks with delayed terminal bridge.
- Extend behaviour with variable schedule of clicks.
- Once behaviour established introduce clickless reward.
- Complete removal of clicks.
- Variable schedule of clickless rewards.
- Fade rewards to scratches, touch and body language with occasional food reward.

It is worth noting that even if trainers only incorporate into their present method of clicker training the delay in the arrival of the food rewards following the click, and provided they are consistent, they will increase the patience of their equine. Increased patience will benefit any clicker-trained equine and will help in the removal of the clicker from training.

CHAPTER 13

How do I use successive approximation?

Successive approximation is the process of breaking down any required behaviour into small manageable steps or learning blocks, and then reinforcing these steps one at a time to create a finished behaviour. The greatest strength of clicker training is the potential accuracy to mark even the smallest desired behaviour. Successive approximation identifies the small steps that a clicker trainer needs to mark in order to efficiently train a horse, donkey or mule. Understanding these two processes makes it easy to see why, when combine, good successive approximation and good clicker training go hand in hand.

Successive approximation is the scientific term for a process that is more easily referred to as shaping. It is important to note that shaping is not just for use with clicker training. Whatever training method the trainer chooses, shaping behaviour and shaping plans will help create success. We all shape behaviour all the time, in all aspects of our lives. We know that general we must learn individual elements of a task before we can progress to performing the whole task. We must first learn to crawl before we can walk. We have to learn the letters of the alphabet before we can make words, sentences, paragraphs, pages and then whole books. We know about shaping. The problem is that we do not know how to do it well, and this creates difficulties when we are training equines.

Shaping behaviour by successive approximation has two elements. The first is the use of a carefully written shaping plan. This plan of training may take twenty minutes to write but cover many weeks or months of training for the animal. The second element of shaping is individual actions that are reinforced during a training session to increase the likelihood of the required behaviour recurring. It is the ability of clicker training to mark these small behaviours, that when combined with a shaping plan, can lead to rapid learning.

Every shaping plan is individual and the structure and content will depend on the current level of training of both the animal and trainer. We must also take into account the individuality of the animal before writing any plan. A nervous animal may require a shaping plan that builds confidence before work on the practical task in question cab be began. An overly confident animal may need to learn to follow the trainer's directions and work through rank order problems before other training tasks can start.

Creating a shaping plan is a written exercise. Often people tell me their shaping plan is in their head. That is not really the place for it. A shaping plan stored in our head is liable to change depending on our mood or time commitments, and this creates inconsistency. If it is just in our mind it is easy for us to skip or miss steps and justify rushing ahead to something more exciting. The shaping plan should be written down, because writing it down provides the following benefits:

- Focus and consistency of training maintained over long time scales.
- The trainer can see how far the animal has progressed during training.
- Breaks in training can occur without the loss of direction.
- Creates more disciplined trainers who are less inclined to skip written steps or to rush the training.
- Allows the trainer to deal with problems by moving back down clearly defined steps to an achievable level, before proceeding again.
- Ensures the trainer does not miss out any vital steps.

The best place to start writing a shaping plan is at the end. Starting with what we want to achieve will influence every step of our plan. The more detail contained in a goal, the more likely we are to include all the necessary steps required to reach the final behaviour safely.

Instead of the goal "I want my horse to load", a more accurate goal for our loading horse might be; to load calmly and willingly into the trailer with or without other horses, in any location, at any time of the day or night and in any weather conditions. To stand calmly while the trailer is made ready for travelling, so that we can happily attend the local show on the 25th May.

Instead of the goal "I want my donkey to have their feet trimmed", a more accurate goal for a donkey that does not like having their feet trimmed by the farrier might be: to stand calmly and willingly, in any location and weather conditions, at any time of the day, while all four feet are calmly trimmed, by the next time the farrier visits on 19th July.

The more detail that can be included in our goal the more information we will have about the number of steps that need to be included. For example, adding 'in any location' to our goal shows us that the animal must be trained in different areas once the animal has learnt to perform the task in one location. The training needs to be repeated in different locations so the process of generalisation can take place and we can be sure the animal has the best chance of success.

Having created a suitable goal we need to work out the first step on our shaping plan. It is remarkably easy to choose where to start if we ask the simple question. Where am I now? The most successful and safest way of starting a shaping plan is to begin with the smallest possible step. It is far better to start with something easy for the animal to achieve, and work through the first steps with ease, than starting with a more challenging behaviour and make a mistake, frighten the animal or have an accident.

For a loading plan, the first step might be ensuring that

leading in general is correct, or even teaching the animal to stand patiently for thirty seconds. If the animal is nervous of walking over a plastic tarpaulin, do not start by working with the tarp. Start by placing a rope or a jumping pole on the ground for the animal to walk over. Discover what the animal is comfortable with and happy to walk over and then make this step the starting point. If the animal cannot walk over a tarp, then they are unlikely to go in the trailer either.

If we were working with a person who had fear of spiders, expecting them to start by holding a spider would be unreasonable, especially if just the mention of the word spider produced a fear response. We should start with getting them to relax when hearing the word spider or when saying the word before we could move to the next step.

Now that we have found where to start and where we would like to finish all we have to do is to fill in the steps in between. I tend to start by creating the second half of the plan first. What do I do once the animal is calmly performing the required behaviour in the initial training location? I take a blank piece of paper and look at my goal, breaking it up into small segments, such as location, time, numbers of people, weather condition etc. Then I list under each heading as many different variables as possible. For example, under location for loading, I might list the normal location for loading practice, and then in the yard, in the field, at the end of the drive, five minutes' drive away, twenty minutes' drive away.

For the farrier problem, if the animal has been trained by just one person then they will need to get used to a second person. This might include having a person stand at the head while we groom, another person running hands all the over animal, a different person grooming, another person handling the animal while the usual trainer stands at the head and, finally different people picking up the feet.

Each element of the goal is a step on the shaping plan, and we can use an unlimited number of steps. The only guide would be to ensure that the steps are small enough to be safe and achievable, but they should be big enough to stretch the animal's comfort zones a little each time. If the steps do not stretch the animal, progress will be very slow, if any is made at all. Having said that, learning should always take place at the animal's pace.

Having written the second half of the plan, I return to my first step and work from there to where the behaviour is happily being performed by the animal willingly and without hesitation in one location and with one person.

A shaping plan for the farrier might start by ensuring the animal was calmly willing to accept being touched in each area of the body all the way down to the feet. We can break the body into segments for shaping, such as hip, tail or dock, stifle or knee, cannon bone, fetlock, coronet band and hoof. Then we progress to moving the feet on the ground and asking the animal to shift their weight to three legs. We might then progress with picking the feet up for progressive time increments, such as two seconds, five seconds, ten seconds, twenty seconds etc.

The steps may seem extremely small and in some cases insignificant, but that is the point. The steps are there to allow the animal to progress easily and logically and small steps achieve this best. Although there seem to be numerous small steps, animals may progress through them at different rates so to go through from five seconds to twenty seconds of holding up feet may only take one ten minute training session. However, a nervous animal may take five sessions to be comfortable with having their feet touched.

It is difficult to exactly perfectly how an animal might behave or where the edge of their comfort zones could be, so progressing in these small steps also allows us to proceed safely.

The shaping plan does not make training less spontaneous or less fun. I think it actually increases our ability to relax during training and enjoy the journey more. As we now know where we are going and what steps we need to get there, we can free ourselves from worries such as, "Am I doing the right things for my animal?"

How to use a shaping plan

If we are to get the most from our shaping plan we need to be able to use it correctly. We should always start each new training session one or two steps below the step where training finished in the previous session. Starting this way means the work at the start of a new session is familiar to the animal. This helps relax them and build on the knowledge gained from the last session. This familiarity encourages the animal and allows them to receive rewards at the start of the session, and a rewarding start increases motivation in the animal during the rest of the session. Starting with simpler steps also allows the trainer to ease into the session and develop concentration and timing while assessing the animal's mood.

While working on the first five steps of a shaping plan it is advisable to start back at the very first step with each new session and progress through the previous steps as quickly as the animal is willing, up to the finishing point of the last session. For example, if we are shaping the animal to have their feet picked up, and we finished a training session on step five, which was touching the hoof, at the beginning of a new session we should go back to step one, touching the hip and progress through touching rump, stifle and fetlock before beginning work on the hoof. With each session, the speed at which we can run through the first five steps increases. Once we have created this secure foundation and progressed past step five we can change to starting just two steps below our previous finishing point.

Before we progress on to a new step, we must ensure that the animal understands what is required for the current step. If we progress too rapidly, the animal will be unclear of the correct behaviour and the behaviour will break down. If we wait too long before progressing, the current behaviour will be more ingrained and difficult to adapt, or extinguish, so training will slow down.

There are two ways to see if the animal is ready to move on. The first is when the animal starts to offer the behaviour of their own free will. This demonstrates they understand what is required of them, as they are seeking reinforcement. The second measure of readiness to progress is when the animal can accept a variable schedule of reinforcement. A variable schedule means the animal will continue the behaviour for a longer period or offer more tries before being reinforced. If we try to go to a variable schedule and the behaviour dies away then it is clear the animal did not know the correct behaviour to elicit the reinforcement.

In most cases, we should only need to practise the variable schedule between two and four times before we try to move to the next step. This does of course vary and depends on the animal, their stage of training, and the difficulty of the required behaviour.

The key to progression is that behaviour strengthens or gets bigger before it changes. If a behaviour receives a reinforcement and the animal understands which behaviour works, when we remove the reinforcement for the behaviour, the animal is sure to work harder to elicit the reinforcement.

Imagine that we are working with an equine that does not like having their feet picked up and we reach the stage where the animal is happy to stand still while their hooves are touched. Technically, we are reinforcing the behaviour of standing still while being touched. Initially, this might only be for three seconds. Once the animal is happy to stand for three seconds, and we put standing still on a variable schedule. Then we remove the reinforcement for three seconds of standing still. If the animal knows standing still works, they will try harder to stand still in order to gain a reward and this might mean they wait for five seconds. If we reinforce five seconds standing still, we progress to the next step.

Timing the reinforcement with this increase in behaviour is crucial if we are to shape behaviour efficiently. If we wait too long, or make the steps too big, the increase of behaviour will not work for the animal and the behaviour we require will actually die away. If we reinforce too soon, the animal will make very little progress in training.

If, while we are trying to move to the next step, we miss the increase in behaviour and the required behaviour dies away, all we have to do is return to a previous step, reward that behaviour to a variable schedule level, and then try to progress again.

Shaping plans do not have to be written in stone, so if we find that one way of eliciting a behaviour does not work then we can try another. We should not chop and change at the drop of a hat but, if we use our intuition, we will know when to try something new. We must give the animal time to think and offer appropriate responses, but if it is clear the animal is struggling to learn the required behaviour it is good to try something else in order to see if that might help. The only limitation to this process is our imagination.

Whenever we move to the next step of the plan, we must relax what we expect from the animal. If the horse is able to stand calmly in an open trailer with plenty of space, we can expect their adrenaline level to rise and them to be more nervous when they are asked to walk through the trailer with the partitions in place. We have to relax the old criteria if we are to avoid putting too much pressure on the animal. As we increase what we ask of the animal it would be unreasonable to expect the same level of calmness or relaxation we had at previous step immediately. We must recognise that learning is difficult, and as we seek increased performance, it takes a little time for the animal to the perfect the new behaviour. If we demand perfection at the new level straight away we may end up making it impossible for the animal to learn what is expected, as too many criteria will lead to confusion.

The first part of the plan, the foundation, is crucial to the success of the rest it. We should not be tempted to skip any of the time and training required in these early stages. Unfortunately, these early steps can be the least rewarding for the trainer. To succeed we must be happy to enjoy the journey and reward the attempt. Generally, as the animal begins to learn, the progression through the steps accelerates to a point where the animal makes huge amounts of progress in relatively few lessons. This is known as learning to learn.

The shaping plan is the single most important practical tool a horseman can use. We all use shaping and we all have shaped behaviour before in one way or another. Shaping is not new, but understanding the process more clearly and using the principles more accurately allows us to communicate with our equines more efficiently and allows them to understand us more easily.

For more information on shaping see www.hartshorsemanship.com and read "How to create and use a shaping plan" from the Ben's books page.

How do I create a behaviour to be rewarded?

In order to elicit the required behaviours for reinforcement during shaping for clicker training there are four methods we can use, targeting, imitation, modelling or free shaping.

Targeting

Targeting is one of the first behaviours I recommend a trainer teaches any equine, not only because it is good for teaching the animal about clicker training and problem-solving but because it can be used in numerous ways throughout the training process.

Once the horse, donkey or mule has learnt to target, the target can be used to assist the animal crossing tarpaulins, walking under bunting or, in time, even into trailers and horse boxes. For many trainers, using a target as a lure is the easiest way to teach behaviours such as lying down or taking a bow. The trainer can move the target so that in order to touch it the animal must perform certain movements which the trainer can mark and reinforce. As the animal is reinforced they learn to perform the required behaviour. Targeting is used with many animals and can be successful provided the trainer has prepared a shaping plan, carefully breaking down the required behaviour into small steps. Despite the potential of targeting, it is worth remembering that a nervous horse is unlikely to follow the target straight into the trailer. They will have to be shaped over other less scary obstacles first in order to build confidence.

With targeting, it is important to remember that only one behaviour can be rewarded at a time. The animal who is touching a low target may not realise the trainer is rewarding them for lowering their head as well. This is where targeting has some limitations as the animal following the target may not be aware the trainer is shaping specific body movements or behaviour.

Imitation

Imitation is a different way of creating behaviour and is something that different species learn and use to differing degrees. There is no scientific evidence to suggest that equines are capable of observational learning. So, it is unlikely they can mimic the behaviour of other equines simply by watching them perform a given task.

They can perhaps learn how to react to stimuli by following a more experienced animal through or over the problem but it is by no means guaranteed. Getting a nervous horse to follow a more confident animal may help the nervous one provide enough behaviour to earn rewards, which will increase their confidence and allow them to succeed. Even using imitation the behaviour will have to be shaped and if the animal is deeply afraid of loading then they will not follow another horse on to the trailer, but they may follow the other horse over poles and tarpaulins so we can shape their behaviour until they are ready to step on to the trailer.

If a young equine has never walked over a large sheet of plastic before they may be a little nervous but are likely to follow their mother if she is happy to walk calmly over the obstacle. Foals can get a lot of their behaviour from their mothers, just as human children get a lot of their behaviour from their parents. So, handling the mare can help the foal in their training.

Modelling

Modelling and negative reinforcement are direct ways to create the desired behaviour. With modelling or negative reinforcement the trainer applies a degree of physical or psychological pressure to the animal which the animal then tries to remove. As the animal removes the pressure individual behaviours are reinforced. Modelling is where equines are pulled into shapes with equipment, such as lead reins and halters. They are forced to step back with a hand pushing into their chest. For a dog, an example of modelling would be having the trainer push the dog's rear down to click and reward for sitting.

I am not entirely convinced about modelling as a training method used in conjunction with clicker training. I feel that sometimes it can lead to equines just waiting to be put into the correct position. Using a lead rope to pull the horse's head down and through their front legs in order to teach them to bow, is not teaching the animal to bow, but is really just teaching the equine to come off the pressure of the head collar. If we want equines to develop problem solving skills and to offer behaviour, other ways of eliciting behaviour may be more successful than modelling.

Modelling may teach the animal to avoid pressure or how to respond to a stimulus but I am not sure that it teaches the animal to offer behaviours freely. Modelling requires the animal to respond to a stimulus, and without that stimulus they do not know what behaviour is required. This is fine provided the behaviour is one for which the trainer is always happy to provide a cue.

Where modelling is used it should not include excessive force or physical prevention of behaviour but should be used to provide additional information to the animal about what they are required to do. Lightness is the key to success and modelling is perhaps best used to guide equines to make the first step in the new direction of a complicated behaviour.

Free shaping

Free shaping is another way clicker trainers can create behaviours in order to reward the animal. During free shaping the animal is rewarded for naturally occurring behaviours and these behaviours are shaped using only the clicker to create the desired finial behaviour. The horse, donkey or mule does not receive any additional information other than the click and the reward. The animal is not lured or forced into the required behaviour. Free shaping is the best way of teaching an equine to think and become responsible for their half of the training process. The animal is totally in control of their movements and progression relies on the thought processes of the animal.

Free shaping is like providing the horse with a puzzle and the only clues are the timing of the clicks and the silence between them. The success of free shaping really relies on the timing of the trainer's clicks, and their ability to break desired behaviours down into small steps that are achievable by the animal. So in teaching the horse to bow, the free-shaping trainer would initially wait until the horse lowered their head a few centimetres before clicking and rewarding. This slight lowering of the head would continue to be marked and developed into a full bow.

To be successful, the free shaping trainer has to be skilled at seeing and marking behaviour. Only with clicker training can trainers use free shaping, as they do not need to have contact with the animal in order to communicate with them. Not even body language is used during free shaping. The process relies totally on the information provided by the clicks to create behaviour in the animal. Free shaping behaviour is very difficult for the trainer but does, in the long, run rely totally on the animal's desire to work for the trainer's rewards.

There is talk between clicker trainers about a new term – micro-shaping. This is where very small behaviours, such as muscle twitches, are marked and rewarded. I do not believe micro shaping is any different to shaping. I believe that taking small steps is just the correct use of shaping, the smaller the steps the better for the animal. So all shaping should be small or micro.

I would suggest that to be successfully shaped, the animal has to be conscious of the movements that they make. Movements such as muscle twitches may not be conscious to the animal or may be overridden by larger corresponding behaviours. Equines are creatures of movement and so clicking for a muscle twitch while the horse is moving their feet or head will mean that the animal is most likely to believe the rewarded behaviour was the movement not the muscle twitch.

Free shaping is excellent at creating a thinking animal that can solve problems and is prepared to offer behaviours with the hope of getting reinforcement. Free shaping develops problem solving and thinking in the trainer because it requires more skill, patience and imagination.

For any equine that has come from a negative or aversive environment, free shaping will initially be difficult. If the animal has never been allowed to offer behaviours freely, they often fear the consequences of their actions. They will as a result offer very little behaviour for the trainer to reinforce. With such animals the first part of the process is to teach them how clicker training works and that they can offer behaviour without fear of punishment. In essence the animal's trust needs to be recreated, and their communication needs to be restarted.

This can take time, but has to be done before free shaping can be used successfully with more complicated behaviours.

As an example of the differences between the training methods we could look at a behaviour like Spanish walk.

Using imitation would involve one animal watching another perform Spanish walk and then beginning to copy the movements. Unfortunately, this is extremely unlikely as there is still no scientific evidence to suggest equines can learn by observation of others in this way. Or perhaps the horse could be taught to copy the trainer's leg movements and then reinforced for high stepping.

Using targeting would require the animal to be trained to touch the target with their knees. Then the target would be gradually raised up, thereby making the animal reach higher for each knee to target touch. Repetitions of the behaviour would then be requested from the animal as the target is drawn forward in front of them, thus creating Spanish walk.

Using modelling or pressure and release would require something like a dressage whip which would be used to irritate the front legs of the animal. As they lift their feet to avoid the irritating stimulus they are clicked and the process repeated until Spanish walk is achieved by tapping alternate legs with the whip

Free shaping requires the trainer to mark small movements of the animal's front legs. These movements might be while pawing the ground or shifting weight between legs. These movements are developed into higher, more pronounced leg action by the process of shaping, until the Spanish walk is achieved.

Which method is best? Well that depends on the trainer's ability to shape behaviour and their timing, as well as on the equine's ability to think and solve problems. Free shaping is best at creating thinking equines but is more challenging for the trainer. Modelling is easier for the trainer and requires the trainer to use less imagination but does not teach the animal to think or solve problems.

They all have their applications and trainers must choose what they want the animal to learn in excess of the actual behaviour they are trying to teach. Modelling may be more suitable for the trainer who wants to control a particular behaviour or to start the shaping of a difficult behaviour. Free shaping is great for those trainers who want to allow their animals to be responsible for their own learning and to develop a partnership between themselves and their horse, donkey or mule. Whatever method is chosen the key to success is being able to write good shaping plans and shape behaviour well during training sessions.

CHAPTER 14

Do I have to click for everything for ever?

Many people have a concern that they will have to click for everything for ever once they start clicker training, but this worry is very quickly dismissed by all clicker trainers. The clicker is a tool for communication, a great way of communicating the tiny details of a required behaviour to the animal. Once the animal understands the communication and performs the behaviour when required, the clicker can be removed.

Punishment and negative reinforcement as aids to equine/human communication are different from positive reinforcement in that punishment is required every time an unwanted behaviour occurs if it to be effective. During negative reinforcement the negative stimulus or the possibility of the negative stimulus has to be present, no matter how lightly, every time the behaviour is required.

If reinforcement is successful in communicating to the animal what is required, the strength of the reinforcement can fade or change as the new behaviour becomes established. Obviously, if an unwanted behaviour is still occurring after months of punishment, the punishment is not working. If punishment has been successful the behaviour would have changed and punishment would no longer be required.

With positive reinforcement, withholding the reward, at the correct stage of learning, actually makes the desired behaviour stronger. If we teach a puppy to sit using a chocolate drop, we do not continue to give the dog a chocolate drop every time they sit for the rest of their life. Firstly, we would have a very fat dog and, secondly, other things take over as reinforcers – sit and get patted, sit and get your leash put on so we can go for a walk, sit and get your leash taken off so you can run around, sit and get you can have your food. The dog may sit dozens of times in a day and not be rewarded, yet the behaviour does not disappear.

With conventional clicker training, removing the clicker has always been possible, but sometimes it is difficult, depending on the individual animal. In fact, quite often, people do not remove the clicker for months after training the behaviour. I have even known trainers to continue using the clicker for a behaviour that the horse had learnt years before.

Getting rid of the clicker

The good news is that the clicker is naturally faded out through the process of shaping behaviour. Imagine a horse that does not like their feet handled. The trainer can use clicker training to shape the behaviour of standing still while being touched. Gradually progressing down the animal's leg to the hoof, and then to moving the hoof on the ground, and then to lifting the hoof for a few seconds. If the animal is nervous, at the start of training they may receive a click and reward for standing still while their neck is touched. As they learn to offer standing still, the trainer may progress to the shoulder and only occasionally reward the neck being touched. From the shoulder the trainer progresses to the top of the leg, now the horse will hardly ever be rewarded for having their neck touched. By the time the trainer reaches the foot, only handling the bottom of the leg will be rewarded, so the clicker is already being faded out of the training process for touching the neck, shoulder, top of the leg. This process should be the same for all behaviours. As training progresses only the newest and most accurate behaviour continues to be clicked and reinforced.

For me, the final stage of getting rid of the clicker completely, starts with the way in which I teach clicker training. In the chapter, "How do I get started?" there is a detailed description of the process I go through when teaching clicker training. I deliberately use this approach because I want to use the clicker to establish the behaviour and then remove it from training as fast as possible.

In my experience, using positive reinforcement seems to accelerate equine learning and aids retention of learned behaviour better than other methods of training. The accuracy of the clicker in communicating to the animal which specific behaviour is required further increases the rate of learning. How fast the clicker is removed depends on the individual animal, and the skill of the trainer. For an animal that is unafraid and capable of problem-solving, the clicker can often be removed from the training of specific behaviours in under two weeks.

The key to rapid removal of the clicker is the use of a terminal bridge, such as the movement of the trainer's hand to the bum bag. This alternative marker signal allows the removal of the clicker much faster than when the clicker is the terminal bridge, as with conventional clicker training.

The next question is, How quickly can food and the new terminal bridge be removed from the training? The answer depends on the trainer's skill at using the variable schedule of reinforcement. Schedules of reinforcement define which behavioural responses will be reinforced and how often. They can be affected by either duration of the behaviour or repetition of the behaviour. A variable schedule of reinforcement means that the number of responses or the duration of the response required for reinforcement varies from one reinforcement to the next.

B.F. Skinner showed that variable schedules are better in several ways than continuous ones.

- Because of its unpredictable nature, variable ratio can keep animals working a long time, so longer sessions are possible.

- More training is possible in a single session because less reinforcement is used for each correct response (especially applicable to food rewards).
- More persistent results.
- Intermittent reinforced behaviours are more persistent and more resistant to extinction. If a response is learned on a variable schedule it seems to be remembered longer and more vigorously.
- More focused training
- Variable schedule can be used to shape behaviour towards a specific goal. The increase in behaviour as a result of withholding reinforcement allows the trainer to select more accurate approximations.

Using a variable schedule of reinforcement, the stronger a behaviour becomes the less often it has to be rewarded to maintain the behaviour at the correct level. Once the trainer has progressed to clickless rewards, the same process is used for removing food as was used with the clicker. The difference is that, because the trainer has already taught the animal to remain patient, through the use of the delayed reward, the complete removal of the food is much easier.

As already explained clickless rewards are rewards that follow the required behaviour, and are marked by a secondary reinforcer such as the movement of the trainer's hand to the bum bag, with no click.

As the animal learns the required behaviour, the trainer consciously withholds the reward and ensures the animal is unable to predict when the reward might arrive. So, when the horse has learnt to pick up each foot calmly for a reward, a variable schedule of reinforcement will be introduced for the feet. In practice, this means that the trainer might reward the first, third and fourth feet but not the second foot. In subsequent sessions the second and fourth leg might be rewarded. After a few sessions the animal might have to wait until the fourth foot is finished before they are rewarded. The other feet might have received a scratch or a stroke but no food. In this way, food can be in a large part removed from training. However, I find it useful to maintain behaviours by occasionally giving an unexpected food reward for a good behaviour alongside normal reward of scratches or physical contact.

We do not have to click for ever, but we do have to understand and use variable schedules of reinforcement while making a conscious effect to remove the clicker and food rewards from training. Sometimes, trainers fear that, if they stop clicking, the previously unwanted behaviour will return or the new behaviour will disappear, so they keep on clicking for months. This is seldom necessary and, even if the behaviour does diminish, all that is required is for the trainer to go back a few steps on the shaping plan and reinforce the required behaviours further, thereby making them stronger, before trying again to remove the clicker or food.

CHAPTER 15

What can I teach with clicker training?

Clicker training is based on the science of behaviour, and as the clicker is a tool that can be used with a primary reinforcer such as food, it can be used to teach everything that the animal is physically and mentally capable of. Equines have been trained for round six thousand years without a clicker and we humans have found ways to teach them whatever we have needed them to know. Clicker training can be used to teach everything that can be taught without a clicker and a few behaviours that it might otherwise be difficult to teach.

In different cultures, all over the world, equines are being trained to do what they need to do, using a multitude of different methods. Their ability to learn is demonstrated by the way they figure out what we want, despite all the different methods of communication. Whether a trainer is successful is not really down to the tools they use, but rather it is in the way they use those tools, combined with their beliefs and the approach they have to training. Clicker training will enhance a good approach to training equines and just confuse a bad one.

A good approach to training equines is a balanced one. I believe that the balance of science and art is the key to success for any equine training. The science of behaviour allows a truthful understanding of the equine mind and the science of learning. The art of horsemanship develops the feel, which allows the practical application of the science. For clicker training to reach its full potential depends on who the trainer is, not what the clicker can do.

A good approach to training is a thoughtful and considered one where the animal always comes first and the science of behaviour is understood and used. Whatever I want to train using the clicker, for me the approach is the same as training without a clicker.

- First identify the individual nature of the equine and human involved to establish if clicker training is suitable for use with this animal, in this environment.
- Then create a detailed goal for the desired behaviour.
- Create a shaping plan.
- Use the shaping plan to begin training and use the clicker to mark the required behaviours.
- Receive feedback during the training process and use this information to refine training and add or remove steps from the shaping plan as required.
- Persist with consistency until success occurs.

For me, all training is about following this simple formula. OK, what the training is and how difficult it might be is more complicated, but this approach to training always works.

If we want to see that my simple approach to training is the truth, we can consider the exact opposite approach to training to see if mine makes sense. The opposite of my approach would be.

- Regardless of the animal's nature or the skills of the trainer deciding to using clicker training, even in an unsafe environment.
- Just start training with no idea what the required final behaviour is or what is required for the animal to learn the behaviour.
- Do not listen to any feedback, adopt the approach that the trainer knows best and just carry on regardless.

- Change directions and behaviours often, and be as inconsistent as possible, give up if the training gets to be hard work.

Common sense tells us that this approach would end in disaster. I believe seeing how absurd it would be to do the opposite of my approach to training should encourage trainers to be a little more structured in their approach.

It is not in the remit of this book to give the details of how best to teach all behaviours that could be taught using clicker training. I believe that each trainer must find their own path to horsemanship so, given the infinite number of possible combinations of equines and trainers, to cover all the possibilities would be impossible. Secondly, I do not believe there is an "ABC" of clicker training. As we have seen in the chapter on shaping, there are a number of different ways any behaviour could be elicited, all using the clicker.

Preparation and writing shaping plans are the key to success with all training and particularly true of clicker training as the animal will learn so quickly the unprepared trainer will struggle to keep up.

Before learning anything else, the horse, donkey or mule has to learn the basic rules of clicker training through either targeting or standing still training and then progress to learning a non-confrontational behaviour. Once the animal has learnt to clicker train, without mugging for food and is safe to handle, then work can begin on whatever the trainer desires.

Teaching general domestication can be done using the clicker. Handling, leading, hoof care, loading, personal space awareness and acceptance of clipping, scary items and preparation for riding. If the animal needs to be able to do it for a safe life in domestication a clicker can be used to teach it.

If the horse, donkey or mule is young and does not have any problems then the trainer, through the use of a shaping plan can teach any required behaviour easily.

As an example, safely teaching a horse to load might require some of the following steps:

- Leading in an enclosed safe area.
- Leading over poles, plastic and pallets.
- Leading under obstacles.
- Tying up.
- Standing still.
- Walking up to the trailer.
- Walking through trailer.
- Standing in trailer.
- Walking through trailer with partitions in.
- Standing in trailer with partitions in.
- Progressive increase of time in trailer.
- Shutting animal in.
- Leaving animal in trailer for up to five minutes.
- Loading in different areas.
- Travelling for five, ten, fifteen minutes.
- Travelling for five minutes unload reload.
- Loading at different times of day.
- Loading in different weather conditions.
- Loading with other equines.
- Loading in a rush.
- Loading with lots of noise and distractions.

When training a horse to load in to a trailer, each one of these twenty-one steps would be further broken down in a shaping plan to create a total of forty-five to fifty-five small steps. Too many trainers rely on the good nature of their animals to get them out of trouble. If we want our young horse to load easily and every time then we need to teach them how to deal with everything that they might encounter before they encounter it. Too many trainers train their horse on Saturday afternoons when everything is calm and relaxed and bright and sunny only to curse the animal because they will not load at 5.30 am, in the dark and rain when everyone is in a rush and frustrated.

Using clicker training is not about going to the trailer with a novice horse and clicking for each step forward, or for touching the target or for each free shaped movement towards the trailer. Yes, we have to do these things at some point in the training, but only when they are going to be safe and easy for the animal to achieve.

If we use clicker training in this way, loading on to the trailer is not an issue. The animal will have done the work first, so that they are confident to follow the trainer wherever they go. It is the same for starting a young horse. If the work is done with the same approach as shown with loading, then putting the saddle on or riding does not require a magic starting method or a special person for starting. The work can be done over the years before the animal ever has to have a rider. It might be sensible to get a fit, sympathetic, careful rider for the first few times, but only to ensure the health and safety of those involved and to give the horse the best chance of success, not because the preparation has not been done and we need a brilliant rider to stay on.

Clicker training can be used for groundwork over poles, plastic and scary objects in general. Standing still and boredom training, where the animal has to stand quietly with the trainer for up to twenty minutes at a time, can also be taught. Obviously, all these behaviours are shaped to create success and safety. All training follows the same pattern: make it easy as possible to start and gradually build up the levels of complexity of the process at a rate that stretches the animal, but does not scare them.

We can use the clicker to train the animal to do tricks. In fact, this seems to be the early appeal of clicker training to many equine owners and trainers. They want to have fun with their animals and show everyone how smart their horses, donkeys and mules are.

Tricks or, rather, novel behaviours are taught with the clicker with ease. Teaching an equine to fetch, carry and play basketball are all possible with clicker training. Positive reinforcement motivates the animal and time spent doing things together can enhance the human/equine relationship.

For me, teaching tricks is the same as teaching any other behaviour and requires, goal, plan, action, feedback, persistence, consistency and success. Writing a shaping plan and shaping the behaviour makes anything from retrieving an object to lying down on command possible. The question is, Why teach these tricks at all? For me, tricks are not just for fun, as we run the risk of turning horses into clowns and I believe that detracts from their spirit and beauty.

In my opinion teaching tricks should have a purpose that is of direct and significant benefit to the animal. I do not believe in teaching circus tricks that are only of benefit to the trainer, so they can say, "Look what I taught my horse to do!"

Teaching trick behaviours can help the animal to develop their problem solving skills, which will help in the rest of their training. Behaviours that are completely novel are most difficult for equines to learn, as they make no sense to the animal. They do not know dropping a ball through a hoop is them playing basketball. After a horse has learnt two or three tricks they learn to learn and the speed of attainment for future tricks becomes quicker.

Tricks might benefit the animal if they are in need of mental stimulation such as when they are on box rest, on limited turn out, or have an injury that prevents full exercise. Keeping the brain working is important to equines, especially if boredom related behaviours are to be prevented. Learning to learn is the reason clicker-trained horses on box rest finish box rest better able to return to training and are usually further ahead in their training than when they entered box rest.

Tricks can help some equines develop mental control and focus so they can choose different, more acceptable behaviour to offer. I worked with a donkey that was deemed aggressive. He would bite and gave threateningly aggressive signals. With clicker training I taught him a range of different behaviours including fetching my hat, carrying a bucket, bowing, smiling and rolling out a red carpet. These behaviours gave him something to do, providing him with much needed mental stimulation, and a way to get the attention he so badly wanted. By teaching him to smile, people's opinion of him changed, from grumpy nasty donkey, to believing he was a smart donkey with a great character. With this change of perception came a change in people's body language and he was, as a result, calmer around people as he would offer a smile rather than a bite for attention. He was seventeen when he started to learn these tricks and, although his difficult behaviour never completely disappeared, he was easy to handle and much safer to be around.

We can also use clicker training to work with emotional development and behavioural problems and those areas are covered much more depth in the next two chapters.

Basically, the trainer's imagination is the only limitation on what can be taught with clicker training. Whether it is teaching new behaviours to young or old equines or getting rid of unwanted behaviours, given the correct environment, and correct use, the clicker is a tool that can help equines learn whatever they need to know. In certain situations the clicker might not be the best tool for the job, as other methods might give additional benefits that would better suit the individuals involved, but the clicker could be used if desired.

CHAPTER 16

How can I use clicker training to solve problems?

Having learnt how to clicker train, we can now discover how clicker training stops a horse from bolting and how it helps with any other equine problem behaviour. The opening chapter in this book, asks if clicker training can stop a bolting horse. The answer is not while they are bolting. However, it also asks a different question, "Can you use clicker training to retrain a horse that bolts?" Then the answer is yes. This small but significant difference in the questions gives us the clue in how we can use clicker training to solve our equine problems.

Trainers find it difficult to imagine how to use positive reinforcement to directly deal with a difficult or unwanted behaviour. ("If the horse is biting, when do I click to stop them biting?") This may be because we grow up observing the very direct approach of punishment, where it is easy to see and understand its application to problem behaviour, even if we disagree with its use.

As with everything else about clicker training, it is unfortunately not as easy as just clicking at the appropriate moment to make the unwanted behaviour stop. Clicker training is just not that powerful. Once the behaviour is occurring there is very little that can be done with the clicker to stop the behaviour apart from throwing it on the floor, distracting the animal and thus stopping the unwanted behaviour momentarily. That is the unfortunate thing about clicker training: there has to be some form of desired behaviour to mark or nothing happens.

So the reason a clicker cannot stop a horse that is already bolting is that there would be nothing to mark or reward.

Some trainers use the clicker and rewards as a distraction to prevent unwanted behaviour. They use the clicker to help the horse concentrate on something other than their perceived fear or area of concern. This can work to get the animal past scary objects but does not deal with the problem constructively for the long term and works only in some circumstances.

The way in which clicker training can prevent unwanted behaviours is by retraining the animal, so that the cause of the behaviour is overcome and therefore the behaviour is less likely to occur.

First we must consider that unwanted or problem behaviours are not really a problem for any equine. Many equine behaviours we consider problems are just the opposite for the horse, donkey or mule. Their perceived problem behaviours are in fact their solutions to the problems that occur in domestication. Every species has a species specific defence reaction, and for equines this is generally to run away. If the animal is prevented from running away they are forced to use biting, kicking, rearing and bucking to solve their problems. Any time we see these behaviours we are seeing the animal communicate something about how they feel about their current situation.

Every behaviour, whether it is wanted or unwanted, serves a purpose for the animal involved. The behaviour is in some way reinforced or it would not keep occurring. So, for clicker training to be effective in dealing with problems, it has to be more rewarding or more motivating than the cause of the unwanted behaviour.

If we take someone with a very bad fear of spiders, and we offer to help them overcome their fear using positive reinforcement. First we establish that they like money, and then we offer them £1 to hold a large tarantula spider. Every person suffering from arachnophobia I have asked this of has looked at me as if I am crazy, of course a pound is not enough reward. So I offer £10, £50, £100 even £1,000, usually with no takers. They say they like money but their fear of spiders if bigger than their desire for £1,000. Sometimes the offer of £1,000,000 is all that would tempt them to try. If we take this back to the horse with the fear of loading, a piece of carrot is not going to be enough motivation to have them overcome their fear and walk on, and ten carrots are unlikely to work either. Even if we walked out with the world's largest carrot and put the carrot in the trailer the horse would be very unlikely to walk up the ramp and happily into the trailer.

We cannot motivate the truly fearful animal to overcome fear with even a large reward so we have to break the phobia down into small steps and ask the animal to work in smaller steps for reasonable rewards. So we ask the person scared of spiders to take one step towards a spider for a £1. For the horse, walking over a rolled up sheet of plastic or just taking a step towards the trailer for a piece of carrot could be the starting point of loading.

Before beginning to work with any equine problem a trainer should try to find the cause. This does not necessarily mean the exact way the animal was mistreated in the past, but just to establish what purpose the behaviour serves.

There are a number of causes of behavioural problems in equines and these include pain, medical conditions, genetics, environmental factors, incorrect nutrition, learned behaviour or past experience, fear, and rank order problems. Problems caused by pain, medical conditions, genetics and nutrition imbalance must be corrected first using the appropriate professional assistance and clicker training can be of very little help directly with these. However, it may be of use with any residual behavioural problems once the initial cause has been removed.

Environmental stress can sometimes be helped by clicker training, although correcting any environmental problems would be my preferred first course of action. By changing the environment, equine problems are often removed completely, but in some cases the remnants of the behaviour may persist and then clicker training may be used. The mental stimulation provided by clicker training can help offset the stress caused by confinement of box rest or limited turn out. Using clicker training to teach the animal confidence and problem-solving may in it self help the animal cope better with a restrictive environment in the short term, but the real solution is to find a better environment for the animal as soon as is possible.

Clicker training is most useful for the behavioural problems that originate from the animal's previous handling and training, from fear, either learned or innate, or from those problems that arise due to a lack of experience and training. Clicker training cannot stop a behaviour while it is occurring and so the only way to use clicker training to remove problems is by retraining the animal to offer more suitable behaviours in the place of unwanted ones.

There are four methods of using positive reinforcement to change behaviour: we can train an incompatible behaviour, reward the absence of a behaviour, we can put the behaviour on a cue or we can change the animal motivation. For any unwanted behaviour, any of the four could be used. The trainer just needs to use their imagination and consider which is best for the individual situation and animal involved.

Train an incompatible behaviour

If the horse, donkey or mule performs an unwanted behaviour we can counteract it by teaching the animal a different behaviour that receives rewards. This new behaviour must be incompatible with the unwanted behaviour. If our horse has learnt to kick the stable door because they are expecting food, we can train the animal to either target an object in the stable or teach them to stand on a rubber mat in order to receive rewards. We can then teach them to offer this behaviour in order to receive their normal food rations.

Standing on the mat or touching the target are incompatible with kicking the stable door, therefore kicking will diminish if the new behaviour is more rewarding than the old one. Teaching an incompatible behaviour has two parts. First the animal must learn the new behaviour. This is taught by shaping the animal's behaviour using clicker training. The behaviour is put on a cue, such as a word or the trainer pointing to the object. The second part of the training requires teaching the animal that the new behaviour can be used to receive food in the stable. This involves placing the target or mat in the stable and asking the horse to touch the target or stand on the mat. When they do, they receive their food bucket. Through repetition the animal learns that banging the stable door is not going to work but more acceptable behaviours do.

The horse will, of course, kick the door during the learning process because that behaviour has been successful in the past, but kicking the door has to be ignored and not rewarded in any way. This process of ignoring the unwanted behaviour is called extinction. Only the new incompatible behaviour can now be successful at receiving buckets of food. The only possible drawback of using the mat for the equine that kicks the stable door is that, because both behaviours involved using their feet, the animal may learn to paw the mat rather than just stand on it.

Standing on the mat or targeting can also be used to prevent horses barging out of stable doors the moment they are opened. If the animal receives a reward for touching the target away from the door or for standing on the mat while the trainer enters the stable they will not be able to barge the door.

Put the behaviour on a cue

This technique requires careful consideration. The premise is that if a behaviour comes under stimulus control, i.e. the behaviour only occurs in conjunction with a cue, then the behaviour will diminish in the absence of the cue. The problem with many unwanted equine behaviours is that they are potentially dangerous and deliberately teaching such behaviours could prove dangerous to the trainer. For example, I would not recommend that a trainer teaches the horse to bite them on cue in order to not give the cue in future!

For this method of training to work, the desired behaviour has to only occur when it is asked for, and it can only be rewarded when it occurs in conjunction with the cue. So a horse that constantly pulls for grass when being led can be trained to graze using the clicker and then this behaviour could be put on a cue. Once fully trained, the behaviour is not rewarded when performed with the cue. The cue can then be withheld when the animal is being led.

Other possible behaviour which might benefit from this approach include pawing the ground, rubbing the head against the trainer or nuzzling the trainer for attention. Care must be taken with this approach and consideration given to the problems that will arise if the behaviour is not fully under stimulus control.

Reward the absence of the behaviour

This is a great way to change behaviour if the trainer does not really want the animal to offer a different behaviour, but just wants them to stop what they are doing. By rewarding other behaviours that are not the unwanted behaviour, the rewarded behaviours will increase, leaving little time, space or motivation for the unwanted behaviours.

Using this method, the trainer does not have to identify a specific behaviour to reward. While working with a two-year old colt who was teething and hence wanted to bite everyone who approached his stable door, I began to stand in front of him, just out of reach, and reward every position of his head that was not towards me. I ignored head positions that were in my direction and rewarded everything that was not biting me. This is different to training an incompatible behaviour where the trainer chooses just one behaviour to reinforce. With rewarding the absence of a behaviour it is almost like teaching the animal a concept of what behaviours are likely to be effective at getting rewards and which ones are unlikely to work.

After a couple of sessions with the biting horse, whenever I approached the stable door he positioned his head away from me in some way and I was able to reward him and safely enter the stable. Following on from that success, I was able to extend the concept of keeping his head away from me while I was grooming him.

A word of caution: equines are smart enough to work out behaviour chains. If the animal nips the trainer and then pulls their head away, and the trainer then rewards the position of the head, the animal is very likely to learn to bite and pull their head away as a means of getting the trainer to click and reward. It is not that they are being deceitful but only that the proximity of the click to the biting indicates to the animal that the biting is part of the behaviour required in order to receive the reward. To avoid this problem, wait for the rewarded behaviours to occur without the undesired behaviours. Secondly, if the unwanted behaviour occurs, wait six to eight seconds from the unwanted behaviour, then clearly mark and reward a more acceptable behaviour.

Change the animal's motivation

This is my favourite method of changing equine behaviour. If we understand the animal's motivation for the behaviour we can change the motivation and the behaviour will change. Many unwanted equine behaviours are motivated by fear or by a belief that the current behaviour is successful at receiving the required results.

If an equine is scared of being clipped and we reshape the behaviour of clipping in small steps so that clipping brings rewards, the animal will be more likely to accept being clipped. If a donkey kicks when the trainer tries to touch the animal's leg this is usually because the animal is scared and has learnt that kicking works. Therefore, if we build trust and confidence between the trainer and animal, soon the donkey will not feel the need to protect themselves and so will not kick out. If the animal believes kicking works at preventing their feet from being handled and the trainer can teach them that standing still and having their feet touched brings rewards they are more likely to offer standing still because they want human contact or food rewards.

This is where shaping behaviour comes in yet again to clicker training. The trainer will have to shape this change in motivation. Much unwanted behaviour is self rewarding or ingrained through repetition. Because we cannot use the world's biggest carrot to motivate the behaviour we must make the behaviour small enough so that on balance any fear or previous conditioning is overpowered by the desire for the food.

So for an equine that is fearful of being clipped we would produce a shaping plan to create a change in motivation. By using the clicker to mark desired behaviours we can help the animal to accept that standing still is a good behaviour and that there is nothing to fear from being clipped.

As a rough guide, the main areas to include in the shaping plan would be as follows but these fifteen steps should be broken down into a further forty-five to fifty-five smaller steps to make the learning easier and less fearful for the animal. This does of course depend on the animal current stage of domestication.

- Teaching standing still.
- Standing still while being touched all over the body.
- Standing still while being touched all over with strange objects.
- Standing still when hearing the clipper.

- Stand still when hearing the clipper and being touched all over the body with the trainer's hands.
- Standing still while being rubbed all over with an electric tooth brush turned off.
- Standing still with electric tooth brush turned on.
- Standing still while touched all over with toothbrush.
- Standing still while being rubbed all over with the clippers turned off.
- Being touched all over the body while hearing the clippers in close proximity
- Standing still while clippers on and touched to back of hand on neck.
- Standing still while clippers on and touched to back of hand on different parts of the body.
- Standing still with clippers on skin on different parts of the body.
- Clipping different parts of the body.
- Clipping all the body.

The progression of each step will depend on the animal's level of fear and the skill of the trainer. See the chapter on "How do I use successive approximation?" to learn more about writing shaping plans.

A fear of loading might be overcome by teaching the animal to walk over and accept other obstacles first, before even reaching the trailer. The advantage of clicker training in these problem-solving situations is that the animal's are learning to offer behaviours for reinforcement and they are learning to solve the problems they will meet in the future. Problem solving with clicker training is not about making the animal stop an unwanted behaviour or making them deal with a scary object. It is about allowing them to learn how to deal with scary objects and when to offer other more reinforcing behaviours.

Using clicker training to solve equine behavioural problems is not a quick fix solution. It is long term and it has countless benefits in so many areas of the animal's life that it is worth taking the time to use clicker training. If nothing else, before choosing how to deal with an equine problem I invite all trainers to ask themselves, how they would like to be treated if they had a fear or phobia. With force as quickly as possible, or with five pound notes and as much time as is required?

CHAPTER 17

Can clicker training be used for emotional development of equines?

Clicker training is based on the science of operant conditioning which requires the animal to understand which behaviours are reinforced and which are not. Unfortunately, it is extremely unlikely that an equine could possibly work out that a click was actually for an emotional state of mind, not for a physical movement. If they could differentiate between physical and emotional responses, it would mean that, for all clicker training and probably all training methods, the animal would have to decide whether their emotional state or physical activity were being reinforced, and that would be truly confusing. It is very human to try and mark an emotional state. We can see the animal relaxing, so we mark what we believe is relaxation and, because we know what we are marking, we believe the animal will too. Despite this, it has become common for trainers to use clicker training to try and develop emotions such as calmness and confidence.

Unfortunately, this approach is misleading. It is clearly impossible to mark true emotions, mainly because we cannot know what the animal is thinking at any given moment, or how they feel at the precise moment of the click.

If a horse is nervous, with their adrenaline raised by a scary situation, and the trainer waits until the animal's adrenaline levels appear to drop and then mark what the trainer believes is calmness, the horse would see it differently. The horse would connect the click to a behaviour such as head lowering because equines are creatures of movement. Behaviours that involve movement are most noticeable to equines and therefore override stationary behaviours or emotions. So, when body movement occurs at the same time as a stationary behaviour, the movement takes precedence in the animal's mind. Potentially if an animal were clicked for standing still, but was swishing their tail at he same time, they may believe tail swishing was being reinforced.

However, despite not being able to directly mark emotions, clicker training can influence the emotional states of equines, by encouraging behaviours that are most commonly found during the required emotional state. It is also true that, because the use of clicker training creates greater problem-solving abilities and confidence, the animal is better able to act calmly in difficult situations.

Emotional development is achieved by working with the animal and allowing them to learn, in a calm, considered way. It is not about teaching special behaviours or being able to mark emotions but rather just working with the animal in the right way to encourage the desired emotional states.

A very physical behaviour that we can teach an equine to offer is standing still. Evolution has determined that for equines standing still when encountering a predator or problem is potentially the least successful way to behave. Unfortunately, in domestication most behaviour of general handling and health care require the animal to stand still even when they are afraid. By shaping the animal's ability to offer standing still, we can develop greater ability to stand still in challenging situations. The animal may still be afraid but they offer standing still in the hope that will solve whatever problem they face.

Standing still is trained from the start of clicker training, and can be increased through gradual exposure to more challenging situations. In this way the trainer will begin to drop the brush during grooming, then start moving the grooming box around. Only standing still is rewarded. The exposure to scary things can continue to increase up to the grooming box being slid under the animal, balls bounced around them etc. This is different from habituation where the animal is exposed to the scary stimulus until they no longer respond to it. When teaching the animal to offer standing still, the exposure to more difficult situations is gradual, and we look for a conscious choice of the animal to offer standing still. It is not a process of scaring the animal and waiting for their fear response to diminish.

By using clicker training and working with the horse, donkey or mule we can develop their confidence. To do this we have to work with them through mildly challenging situations and allow them to learn that they can deal with the problem.

Many trainers use scary obstacles to teach equines to cope with scary situations they may encounter. If a trainer applies enough pressure to the animal, it is relatively easy to make even a scared horse walk over a piece of plastic sheet. When trainers use pressure halters and thin rope head collars to make a horse deal with a scary situation they do indeed *make* the animal walk over the plastic. The animal has very little choice and learns that the trainer is able to make them do things they find scary. Yes, the animal has learnt to go over this plastic in this location with this trainer. But that is all.

If we work with a horse, donkey or mule and to allow it to learn that they can deal with the problem they face, they learn confidence and problem solving. This is achieved by gradual exposure to the scary object and rewarding forward behaviour. Whether we use clicker training or other methods of positive reinforcement to achieve this does not matter. By allowing the animal to learn they can cross the plastic in a relaxed calm way, we teach them to deal with other problems. In effect we begin to give them information on how to deal with other scary situations whenever and wherever they occur.

As I have stressed before, every equine is different and some are bolder than others, so how each animal's shaping plan develops with depend on the individual situation. The trainer may have to keep the nervous animal facing the obstacle at a distance in order for the animal to deal with it in tiny steps. If the trainer did not encourage the animal to deal with the problem they would just choose to run away. It is as if the trainer believes in the courage and abilities of the animal even when the animal does not.

The difference between force and choice is allowing an equine to learn what they can do for themselves. By overcoming obstacles with the trainer we develop a more confident animal that does not have to spook, shy and bolt at the things they meet on a hack.

Relaxation can be encouraged by training the animal to stand still and be bored for longer and longer periods of time. If we mark standing still and head lowering we are likely to encourage those behaviours. Sometimes, when offered a food reward, a tense, fearful animal may not take it and if they do they may not chew it. If this is the case we use scratches instead of food rewards. Scratches can relax the animal further because of the effects of scratching on lowering heart rate.

Increasing the animal's confidence and problem solving skills increases the animal's ability to relax in different situations and builds confidence in the trainer. All of this work with difficult and challenging situations has the side effect of developing trust between trainer and the animal, providing the trainer is consistently calm. Both equine and human will have a greater understanding of how the other works and how they will react in different situations and this ability to predict the behaviour of each other is the foundation of trust.

Clicker training's use of positive reinforcement can have

the benefits of consciously developing equine emotional states of confidence, relaxation and trust as well as enhancing the mental skill of problem solving, but these have to be achieved through good training practices and through exercises where the equine can learn the appropriate behaviours which in turn lead to improved emotional development.

CHAPTER 18

Can clicker training be used in riding?

One of the difficulties people have with clicker training is making the transition to using it with ridden work. The main reason for this may be because a ridden clicker lesson is completely different in structure to anything trainers are used to seeing with equines.

When we work on the ground with clicker training, we understand that we need to reward behaviours and that the interruption of behaviours in order to give the reward is part of the process. Once the behaviour is learnt and the clicker removed, training is not so disjointed.

However, the normal image of ridden work is of the fluid use of aids for the continuous repetition of behaviours through the use of negative reinforcement. With traditional ridden work, a thirty-minute session can be continuous and transitions between different elements are seamless. Even if the horse is allowed to stretch out for a minute or two they still continue to walk afterwards. For this reason I think equine owners and trainers can view the ridden clicker lesson with a degree of confusion and concern.

As we have seen, the click marks a behaviour we want to repeat. With traditional aids, the release of pressure from the bit, leg or seat, negatively reinforces the behaviour we want the animal to repeat. One of the differences in clicker training is that following the click we have to stop the training in order to reward the animal. So to use clicker training in the saddle we have to first accept that the lesson will stop and start just as with ground work. The key is to keep in the back of our minds that everything we do is working towards removing the click altogether. So, when we are using the clicker to teach a ridden exercise, we know that we are teaching a behaviour in a way that means the clicker will not be needed in the future. If we change how we view learning we can begin to accept the differences in ridden clicker training.

Potentially, the different shape of the lesson may be very beneficial to learning, with small segments of accurate information positively reinforced and the equine having time to process the information before being asked for the next repetition. In essence we have to understand that we first teach the behaviour before we ask for fluid repetition.

One of the other difficulties trainers find when they want to clicker train ridden work is how to hold the clicker. Using a button clicker rather than a conventional thumb only clicker can help as the rider's thumb does not have to be in the clicker continuously. The button clicker can be taped to the end of a piece of wooden dowelling rod. This can be carried in the rider's hand much the same way as a whip. Alternatively, the clicker could be taped to the handle of a whip for the same purpose. I would suggest the whip is not used as a whip during the clicker training session as the combination of punishment and food reward could create conflict in the horse's mind. Finally, the clicker could be attached to a wrist coil, so the rider can hold it in the palm of their hand yet still let go of it if they need to. Whatever the chosen method of carrying the clicker, I would suggest that the rider gets used to its feel during some ground training sessions before taking it up into the saddle.

Using traditional, click-and-reward-every-time training, there can be a lot of stopping and starting. With my method of clicker training, using the intermediate and terminal bridges, the training can become more fluid. However, the trainer does still have to be good at using variable schedules of reinforcement in order to phase out the use of the clicker completely.

If the horse has been taught on the ground that the click is a "keep going' signal it means that it can be used in the saddle in a similar way. So a twenty metre circle can be broken down into small segments and shaped with the click for specific movements, and the movements of the trainer to retrieve the reward, or the shift of weight to get the animal to stop, becomes the terminal bridge. The horse will feel the weight changes and whenever we click and then stop to give the horse a reward the animal learns that stopping always precedes a reward. Asking the horse to stop and reaching for the reward from the bum bag becomes the terminal bridge for the horse. For this to work, stopping or reaching to the bum bag has to coincide with a behaviour the rider wishes to reinforce. In practice the animal learns to listen to the clicks and, provided reaching for the reward is often only a few seconds from the last click, stopping does not have to coincide with a behaviour for the animal to figure out what is required. The animal seems capable of learning about the required behaviour just from the accuracy of clicks and the variable schedule of reinforcement.

As the clicker is faded out through the use of variable schedule of reinforcement, just as it is on the ground, the movement of the rider to retrieve the reward can still act as a terminal bridge until food rewards are removed completely, except for the occasional reward to maintain difficult or infrequently used behaviours.

The clicker can be used to help the horse ride up to scary objects. This behaviour should ideally be shaped first by leading the horse over and up to as many challenging objects as possible during ground clicker training sessions. Then the horse can be long lined over the same obstacles. Many horses are happy to be led over and up to scary objects, as they are following their trainer, which gives them confidence. However, in riding, the horse must meet the obstacle first with no trainer to follow. For this reason, long-lining can be a very useful step to helping horses that spook at new or scary objects, as they learn to meet the problems first but they can still see the trainer. Once the horse is comfortable with this, then the clicker can be used in the saddle to shape the horse's progress towards the scary object. Steps towards the object can be rewarded, but the animal will still need time to gently approach the object and relax a little before taking the next step. This is the process of systematic desensitisation, which is the same on the ground or in the saddle. Systematic desensitisation is the gradual exposure of the animal to a scary object while ensuring the animal relaxes before the next increase of exposure to it.

Whether leading, long-lining or riding when rewarding movement in the horse, I believe it is extremely useful to delay the arrival of the food reward until the animal has taken a few steps after the click. This way the horse does not hear the click and stop suddenly in anticipation of the reward. Obviously, the number of steps following the click should be subject to a variable schedule of reinforcement. This way the duration of behaviours can be increased by the addition of second and third clicks before the food reward is given. The extra few steps and delay of the reward also prevents the overly enthusiastic horse stopping so sharply from the trot that the rider is dumped over the horse's shoulder.

It is impossible to ride without applying some form of pressure to the animal. The release of this pressure either through the bit or the legs also marks correct behaviours through negative reinforcement. Clicker training can help the animal learn what is required of it in order to minimise the amount of pressure that is required from the rider's aids. This way the aids remain as cues for behaviour. Once the click is removed, any release of pressure will continue to mark the desired behaviours. Care must be taken not to use force or pain in conjunction with clicks or food rewards.

If the animal has a ridden problem the rules are the same as for problems on the ground. The trainer must shape the behaviour rather than going straight to the problem. Depending on the animal's level of fear, trying to click to get the horse across the stream they are clearly terrified of may not be effective. However, shaping the behaviour will create a real chance of success.

The shaping process may start with ground work and long reining before ridden work finishes off the process. This also minimises the need to use the clicker in the saddle. My experience has been that the more preparation is done on the ground then the sooner the clicker can be removed once in the saddle. Learning to learn is an equine ability which is a great asset to the training process, and if behaviours are taught from the ground first, without the rider's weight to hinder movement, animals may find it easier to offer behaviours that can be shaped. Once on the horse's back the rider can give aids or previously established cues in order to elicit the behaviour from the horse.

If we have a horse that bolts then the trainer must identify why the animal bolts. Quite often if we can teach the animal to offer standing still as a response to scary situations we gain control over their flight mechanism. Clicker training also develops the equine problem solving skills, helps to develop confidence and creates trust, all of which could easily help the animal to deal with the situations that previously had caused them to bolt. By introducing the animal to situations that would normally raise their adrenaline and initiate bolting we can shape their behaviour to get them to remain calm and relaxed. This only works if they are not overexposed to the situation too early on during retraining and that their motivation for the food is not overridden by the desire to run away.

Learning to use the clicker in the saddle is largely a matter of practice and trial and error, and responding to the feedback the animal gives the rider. It is about the animal learning the required movements and the appropriate responses to the rider's aids so that the rider does not have to click for ever. Clicker training in the saddle swaps the fluid nature of traditional pressure and release training for an initially more clunky start-stop training session but if it is done carefully, the horse can progress rapidly through to the removal of the clicker and on to the finished behaviour.

CHAPTER 19

What else do I need to know about clicker training?

What if my equine is not motivated by food?

Due to the restriction in the variety of their diet, it is rare for domesticated equines not to be motivated to some degree by food rewards. Different foods may differ in their value to different animals and therefore have different motivational effects on the animal's rate of work. It may be a matter of experimenting with a variety of different foods to find ones that are most valued by the animal. A mixture of rewards during a session can also help maintain the animal's motivation. Motivation for different food rewards will change throughout the day and vary at different times of the year depending on the animal's environment and management.

Trainers often say their animal is not motivated by food because they compare the rate of work for rewards of their animal against that of an extremely food motivated equine. Depending on each animal's confidence levels, trust in the trainer, and their problem solving ability their response to any sort of training will vary. Trainers tend to think that because food and positive reinforcement are involved the animal should be extremely keen to work. However, if the training is difficult, makes little sense to the animal, if the animal fears the consequences of mistakes or is required to deal with a fear or phobia then they may not be very motivated to work, even if they are normally motivated by food. Sometimes one animal will just have a slower, more considered response to food rewards and the trainer will have to accept a slower rate of response.

If an equine appears unmotivated by food in a particular task, it is worth trying different foods and changing the task to something easy and non-confrontational, in an attempt to increase the animal's motivation. Changes in the timing of clicker training sessions to coincide with times when the animal will be most eager to receive rewards may also help, but I do not recommend withholding food from any equine to make them hungry for clicker-training purposes. If changes in reward type and work fail to increase the animal's motivation and the animal will not work at all for any food rewards then using scratches as a reward can be a very useful alternative to food.

What if my equine does not appear to like scratches?

Any equine's motivation and enjoyment of scratches will vary due to a number of factors, including the time of year, weather conditions, their individual confidence and relationship with the trainer. Most equines in a herd situation will engage in mutual grooming at some time, and they will also rub against a tree or fence to alleviate an annoying itch. However, scratches from humans can be a totally different matter, with nervous or fearful animals being unable to relax enough to enjoy scratches, in which case either food should be used as a reward or the trainer must first work using other methods to encourage confidence in the animal. To be most successful as a reward the animal must have first learnt that scratches are a good thing to receive from a human. Following the acceptance of scratches, the location of the animal's favourite itchy spots must be found through trial and error and by varying the pressure of scratches to find the optimum for each animal. If necessary, a rubber massager can also be tried to help create a sensation the animal will enjoy.

Are there any behaviours that should not be taught to an equine?

The basic rule here is to use common sense by thinking through what will happen if a particular behaviour is offered in a different circumstance. One of the behaviours I least like to see an equine taught, is "shaking hands". Firstly, it is circus trick that humanises the equine. Secondly, if the animal raises their feet for "shaking hands" during other times, such as when the trainer is trying to pick up feet, while stood with the trainer or while in the stable, the trainer can be kicked or even struck on the head and the animal can learn to paw or kick stables for attention. I would also avoid teach any equine to "count" by pawing the ground as this can escalate and be generalised in to so many other annoying behaviours. Teaching the equine to kiss is another "cute" behaviour that personally I feel is for the fulfilment of the trainer's emotional needs. If the animal finds "kissing" the trainer's face effective at receiving rewards it is likely to try it with other people and this is where the danger lies. For me if trainers want to kiss their horse fine, but don't teach the horse to kiss people, just in case!

I would not teach an equine to "play football", using their feet to kick the ball, as they can generalise this action to kicking other objects or striking out at people's knees. If a trainer wants to teach "playing football" then I always suggest teaching the animal to use their nose to push the ball around. Although this is not without the risk of making the animal more pushy and inquisitive, at least this behaviour is potentially less destructive than using the animal's feet.

Can I clicker train more than one equine on the same yard?

Many trainers ask this question. They are keen to know if a clicker-trained horse hears clicks while they are shut in the stable will they learn completely random behaviour. They also want to know if listening to a clicker training session can frustrate their equine if they are not involved.

The simply answer is that different equines can be trained within earshot of each other. They very quickly learn to recognise when food rewards follow clicks and can identify when they are being clicker trained. They do not, in my experience, learn random behaviours which occur while another animal is being trained.

A clicker-trained equine that has to stay in their stable and watch other animal being trained in front of them can show signs of frustration or excitement.

This is possibly just due to the stimulus of food triggering the horse's motivation to work as it would do in any situation. As they learn that clicker training is only available in some situations and not others, and provided any excitement is not rewarded, this usually diminishes but never completely disappears.

What if I click the wrong behaviour?

Clicking the wrong behaviour is a common worry of new clicker trainers, as they fear the animal will learn an unwanted behaviour. It is inevitable that during the course of training the timing of a few clicks may not be as accurate as they should be. One click for the wrong behaviour does confuse the animal and slow down learning, but it is not difficult to overcome. Unfortunately, the animal does not learn to perform the correct behaviour with just one click, so they are unlikely to learn an unwanted one with just one click either.

If a trainer recognises they have clicked the wrong behaviour there is only one way to tell the animal "Whoops sorry!" This is done by not marking or rewarding further repetitions of the unwanted behaviour. If the trainer waits until the animal offers the unwanted behaviour again and this time ignores the behaviour it will diminish through the process of extinction. As the animal discovers this particular unwanted behaviour is no longer rewarded they will offer different behaviours from which the trainer can restart the process of successive approximation. All the trainer has to do is to wait and trust the animal will return to previously reinforced behaviours.

It goes without saying that the more clicks an unwanted behaviour receives the more often the animal will offer that behaviour. If a trainer clicks the same unwanted behaviour four or five times it will become more resistant to extinction. A common problem with teaching horses to pick up their feet is clicking just as the animal snatches the foot back. If this mistimed click is repeated several times the animal learns to snatch the foot back from the trainer. To overcome this, go back down the shaping plan and re-establish an earlier behaviour and then work back up again, this time rewarding earlier, while the foot is still calmly in the air. So, one click in the wrong place is not really a problem but repeated clicks for the wrong behaviour will increase the animal's repetition of an unwanted behaviour. However, even if an unwanted behaviour is reinforced several times it still can be removed, the time it takes just increases proportionally to the number of times it has been mistakenly reinforced.

What do other equine owners think about clicker training?

There is a mixed response to clicker training by the equine world, at one extreme are the total devotees who do not believe that any other method is acceptable. At the opposite end of the scale are the complete disbelievers who are convinced that food rewards have no place in equine training. Between these two extremes lie many individual opinions of clicker training and varying thoughts on its effectiveness and its side effects.

Clicker training has a growing reputation for being either fantastic or terrible depending on the results individual trainers have achieved. The new clicker training enthusiast may well encourage everyone to have ago and tell a potential new trainer how easy clicker training is. On the other hand, it is not unusual for clicker trainers to be met by sceptical comments or even complete rejection of clicker training as a training system.

In most cases, peer pressure comes from those who do not fully understand the process of clicker training and have perhaps only had limited exposure to it being used correctly. It is always unwise to succumb to such peer pressure when training equines, whether it is positive or negative.

Another source of conflict is people who feel threatened by other people using clicker training. It is a human trait to justify our own beliefs. If a trainer is using punishment-based training they may find it easier to attack clicker training rather than reconsider their own training methods more carefully. Just because a trainer has decided to use clicker training they should not presume everyone will be thrilled for them. The answer to these potential conflicts is to let the clicker to do the talking. Clicker trainers just need to understand the process well and use it effectively in the right situations and the success that it brings will silence the critics.

What if the horse, donkey or mule becomes over excited or frustrated through the use of clicker training?

I have met quite a few equines that through the use of clicker training have become overly excitable during training sessions. Some male horses even seem to become sexually stimulated by the process. It is difficult to isolate why this should happen, but it is possible that highly-food-motivated individuals become over-stimulated, and the levels of hormones and brain stimulation causes signs similar to those of sexual excitement to be exhibited. The behaviour may be conditioned by either poorly timed clicks or by a trainer clicking during two simultaneous behaviours. If the trainer is trying to reward picking up feet and at the same time there is movement of the hips or dropping of the penis the horse may believe the movement of hips to be the key to success or the click could be classical conditioned to sexual arousal. Whatever the reason for the development of this behaviour, it can be dangerous and limits the animal's ability to concentrate on the training.

What does seem clear is that the longer the clicker is used and the less patience the animal has, the greater the chance of over excitement. One of the reasons we refined equine clicker training in the way laid out in this book is to create patience and to remove the clicker as quickly as possible from training. These two factors drastically reduce the occurrence of frustrated or sexually orientated behaviour. If the animal has learnt to stand patiently for reward, levels of pleasurable hormones are likely to be kept to acceptable levels, and there is less chance of over stimulation problems. By removing the clicker as quickly as possible from training we prevent the establishment of deeply ingrained, classical conditioned responses before they can develop.

If a trainer is faced with a horse that has already become overly stimulated by clicker training then I recommend immediately stopping clicker training as a matter of safety. Removing the clicker and using a combination of positive reinforcement in the form of scratches and negative reinforcement to train any required behaviours should reduce the levels of excitement almost instantly. It may still be possible to use food rewards, although this will depend on the individual animal. After several weeks with no clicker training it may be interesting to try a small session to see if the behaviour has in anyway diminished. With some horses it may be possible to restart clicker training at this point, using the methods laid out in this book. For other equines it may take a year or more of other methods of training and work before clicker training can be attempted again.

Can I over use clicker training with my horse?

Despite the positive nature of clicker training and its effectiveness at creating thinking equines, I believe that clicker training can actually be a very controlling method of training. If the clicker is used constantly to create all behaviours and is never removed from training then I think it is possible to over train the animal.

Clicker training has suddenly opened up a micro world of behaviour for a trainer to manipulate. Aggressive horses can be trained to put their ears forward regardless of whether they are still feeling aggressive or not. The position of the animal's head when it is standing next to the trainer can be constantly dictated. In fact, with clicker training the trainer can control and manipulate every tiny part of the animal's body to a much greater degree than most training methods.

If the animal is always being clicker trained to high degrees of perfection, I believe that the animal can end up constantly offering behaviours whenever they are in the trainer's presence, in the hope of receiving rewards. This constant behaviour offering poses questions. Does the animal enjoy performing continuously in this controlled manner? Do the demands of always having to offer behaviour whenever the trainer is present put stress on the horse, donkey or mule?

Part of the desire for us to have equines is that they can exhibit their own behaviour and through this create a relationship with us. An over clicker trained horse is similar to a human child that is constantly trying to please everyone, so they perform all the time in the hope of praise or affection. Their behaviour is not really who they are, it is manufactured to be rewarded. In equines, this continuous offering of behaviour would also mean that they could never really relax in the presence of the trainer and this must have a detrimental effect on the relationship between the two.

How do I know if a horse is over-trained? Horses that start to offer behaviours the moment they see the trainer, and continue to offer behaviours, regardless of whether they are reinforced, could be over-trained. If the horse offers ridged unnatural stances when the trainer is present, these could also indicate over training. If the animal shows they have persistent difficulties relaxing around people and there seems to be difficultly in reading the animal's behaviour and connecting with the animal, the animal is perhaps trying to constantly receive rewards and may be over-trained.

As with all training methods, it is a matter of balance between training the animal to offer the required behaviours when they are asked and allowing the animal to relax in the company of the trainer when they are allowed to just be themselves without having to perform. The use of a simple signal such as a bum bag can help prevent over-training as the animal can clearly see and smell when rewards are available and when they are not.

Inevitably, when people first start clicker training they become over-excited and use it a lot. This is different from continually using it to reinforce the same behaviours in the horse for months or years. The potential to over-train a horse is really dependent on two things. One is the personality of the animal involved. An animal that is submissive and low in the social structure of the herd may find clicker training so rewarding that they prove very keen to learn and lead the trainer into a situation where they over-train the animal. The other factor is the trainer's ego and personality. If showing everyone how much their horse, donkey or mule can do is the trainer's major goal then there will be a tendency to over use clicker training.

Horses for me are at their least beautiful when forced to perform endless tricks for the self-gratification of the trainer, and whenever they are tense and continually manipulated to perform I feel they lose their spirit.

CHAPTER 20

What is the future of clicker training?

Peering into the future is a difficult occupation, but I think we can make a start by looking at how clicker training is evolving generally and examining some parallels in the dog world. It seems to me that clicker training is catching on in the dog world in a big way. In the sixteen years since it was bought to the dog world by Karen Pryor and Gary Wilkes it has spread from pet dog owners and enthusiasts into professional canine organisations such as rescue centres and dog charities. It seems to have become the preferred training method for service dogs such as guide dogs, hearing dogs and canine assistants.

Clicker training dogs has taken off for displays of dancing dogs and trick trainers. It is slowly moving into the more competitive world of obedience and showing. Once it is accepted in the commercial dog world, clicker training will have conquered just about the entire dog training world. This is not to say that other methods are not used separately or in conjunction with clicker training: they are and I suspect will continue to be used, because that is the nature of humans. There is always a huge variation in our methods of achieving the same thing.

For the rest of the animal-training world, clicker training is a few years behind the acceptance it is finding in the dog world. It is used in many areas of animal welfare and husbandry. Its use in commercial organisation such as zoos, wildlife parks and welfare organisations will go a long way to validating it as an acceptable method of behaviour modification. It stands to reason that clicker training will continue to spread throughout the animal behaviour and training world. Clicker training has come a very long way from the work of B. F. Skinner with pigeons and rats and has returned full circle to the Brelands' early commercial training with farm animals and their attempts to get it to be used in animal shelters.

So what does the future hold for clicker training horses? In some ways the development of clicker training may follow a similar pattern to these other species. Certainly, clicker training is no longer the underground organisation it was eight or nine years ago. It has reached the mainstream of pet horse ownership. It is even being used in equine rescue and rehabilitation charities. However, it has not really reached the commercial world of equine competition.

To develop further, clicker training will have to prove it can have a commercial advantage to competition yards and trainers around the world. When I was in America, I worked with a horse that had been abused by the training methods used in preparing Arabian halter horses for showing. I helped this horse work through his problems and to be a horse again. When I visited his former trainer, he explained that he knew the methods were hard on the horses and even brutal at times and that he would be happy to change but only if I could keep him winning, because winning is what kept him in business and fed his family. Unfortunately, at the time I knew there had to be a better way of achieving what he wanted, but I did not know what it might be. This happened just a few months before I first read *Don't Shoot the Dog* by Karen Pryor and started to learn about clicker training. I now know clicker training could so easily help many types of competition horses, but the question is, Do the trainers want to use it? Only time will tell. However, I am ready to go back and show that trainer how to train his horses without the whip.

There is a difference in the training of equines compared to other animals. Equines are large flight animals that we sit on, and they can be owned and trained by anybody with money. The species differences between dogs and equines surely means we must make some changes to the way we use clicker training with equines. I think clicker training is still in its evolution in the equine world. We are still learning what works best for our horses, donkeys and mules. That means that clicker training could become even better, with greater potential for helping equines deal with their life in domestication.

There are some potential obstacles to clicker training becoming a widely accepted and valued method of training equines and, if we are to progress, we must avoid them. The British Horse Society has been invaluable to the education and training of hundreds of thousands of young men and women throughout the UK. Its methods of training horses rely on negative reinforcement and punishment. If the BHS does not at some point recognise the place of the science of behaviour and positive reinforcement in training equines then there will be generations of horse trainers still with "the teach him a lesson, he's just being naughty" attitude. If the BHS is brave enough to take on well taught clicker training into the mainstream of the equine education who knows where clicker training could end up.

The equine training world, for some reason, has a tendency to embrace methods which it drops a few years later. This may be because methods are always corrupted by their users. The trainers that originated certain methods of "natural horsemanship", whether we agree with them or not, had an approach to training equines worked for them. They could get equines do what they wanted. However, the more disciples, followers and associates these trainers gathered, the more their methods become adapted and changed by its users.

These methods are the product of invention and while they are subject to the laws of behaviour they are not based on these laws. Clicker training should be different as it is based on good scientific principles, it does not belong to one person and it should be easy to replicate its scientific application time and time again.

Unfortunately, clicker training could fall victim to the same problems as other methods. The laws and principles of behaviour are largely established and in most cases provable, therefore any adaptations should also be based on sound scientific principles. Sadly, this is not always the case. As people get excited about the potential of a better relationship with their equines through the use of clicker training, adaptations and mistakes are already being made. People who have only been clicker training a few weeks are, in their enthusiasm, teaching other people how to clicker train and like a game of Chinese whispers, clicker training is becoming diluted and misused.

The third threat to clicker training is that, by its incorrect use, someone could be seriously or even fatally injured. If one of those people who have chosen to use it after only a few minutes, instruction were to have a serious accident it would give every conventional trainer, magazine and sceptic carte-blanche to write off clicker training as dangerous and not suitable for equines.

Whether the future of clicker training is a bright and successful one as it should be, or it is limited to a fad of well meaning trainers, depends on whether its enthusiasts use it well or whether it is sold on as magic by unscrupulous trainers quick to see an opportunity to exploit people's desire to better communicate with their horse, donkeys and mules. Clicker training is a fantastic method of training equines. I only hope that this potential to improve the equine training world is not lost because people do not take the time to study and learn the truth about clicker training.

As I have deliberately said throughout this book, the clicker is just a communication tool. It is not a replacement for good horsemanship, sound knowledge or experience and the responsibility for whether it is successful or not rests purely with the hands that hold the clicker and, their application of the art and science of clicker training.